JUSTICE TO FUTURE GENERATIONS AND THE ENVIRONMENT

Law and Philosophy Library

VOLUME 40

Managing Editors

FRANCISCO J. LAPORTA, *Department of Law,*
Autonomous University of Madrid, Spain

ALEKSANDER PECZENIK, *Department of Law, University of Lund, Sweden*

FREDERICK SCHAUER, *John F. Kennedy School of Government,*
Harvard University, Cambridge, Mass., U.S.A.

Former Managing Editors
AULIS AARNIO, MICHAEL D. BAYLES†, CONRAD D. JOHNSON†,
ALAN MABE

HENDRIK PH. VISSER 'T HOOFT

Professor Emeritus,
Utrecht University,
Utrecht, The Netherlands

JUSTICE TO FUTURE GENERATIONS AND THE ENVIRONMENT

KLUWER ACADEMIC PUBLISHERS
DORDRECHT / BOSTON / LONDON

A C.I.P. Catalogue record for this book is available from the Library of Congress.

ISBN 0-7923-5756-6

Published by Kluwer Academic Publishers,
P.O. Box 17, 3300 AA Dordrecht, The Netherlands.

Sold and distributed in North, Central and South America
by Kluwer Academic Publishers,
101 Philip Drive, Norwell, MA 02061, U.S.A.

In all other countries, sold and distributed
by Kluwer Academic Publishers,
P.O. Box 322, 3300 AH Dordrecht, The Netherlands.

Printed on acid-free paper

Printed in the Netherlands.

TABLE OF CONTENTS

PREFACE

The analysis of justice between generations proposed in this book is based first of all on a critical reading of Rawls' theory of justice, but it also pays attention to the existential and cultural context of our intuitions about intergenerational equity. Although the desire for justice supplies an independent reason for action, the unprecedented character of the context in which that reason must operate necessarily raises the question of its psychological support: we want justice for future people, but what interest do we have in their welfare in the first place? I have tried to capture this double orientation by making use of Thomas Nagel's conceptual dichotomy between the objective, detached point of view, and the subjective (in our case: the cuturally and historically situated) perspective. There is, on the one hand, a desire for justice that tends towards the definition of transhistorical standards, detached from the particular values of the time and place; there is, on the other hand, a motivational background that is tied to our present position in history, and nourished by the values we presently believe in. I have attempted to bridge the gap between the one and the other dimension by different conceptual avenues, the principal one being a time-related interpretation of Rawls' concept of equal liberty: justice wants us to maintain the worth of liberty over time by perpetuating the conditions of its meaningful exercise. So the values that depend on trust in an open time horizon for us all become a part of the picture of justice itself. But this conceptual linkage does'nt suppress the potentially conflictual character of Nagel's dichotomy, such as I make use of it here. The view of justice, the detached view, suggests an environmental measuring-rod that is valid over time; whereas we know that the standards we project into the future depend on specific cultural options and are subject to historical change. I think it would be wrong to assume that the answer lies in a minimalist position orientated on mere physical survival. It is true that in taking this position, we already have a full agenda, considering the present state of the world, but much more may be involved in order to guarantee an acceptable measure of social and cultural continuity. Moreover, because of its global impact, the future generations issue cannot be faced in political reality apart from the contemporary search for a greater equality in welfare between North and

South. So we cannot step outside our own conceptions of the good life - outside our own position in history. The final challenge is how to generate, or articulate, a common interest of mankind in its own future, that is able to resist the scepticism caused by the modern obsession with cultural relativity and historical change.

Another point made by the present book is that we need to start with a theory like Rawls' in order to be able to stipulate, and develop, the concept of a just basic structure of society. Justice to future generations can be no real proposition unless we accept its overriding priority within the domestic and the international spheres. This generates a fascinating challenge for our legal systems.

My experience has been that the subject, which I considered at first from the sole angle of jurisprudence, draws one forcefully into more adventurous directions such as existential analysis, the philosophy of value or even straigthforward metaphysics. I am aware of the tentative nature of my excursions into that unfamiliar territory.

The subject has been with me for a long time, and probably will be for some more time to come. I have drawn inspiration from many sides. My indebtedness to other writers on the subject is made clear in the book itself. But many other acknowledgments are due. Let me mention first of all the colleagues and students at the philosophy of law seminar at Utrecht University, with whom I discussed the subject several times. Lectures in such different places as Antwerp, Bremen, Brussels, Djokjakarta, Edinburgh, the Hague, Knoxville (US), Paris, Tokyo, Utrecht or Willemstad (Curaçao) provided opportunities for a fruitful exchange of ideas. The same goes for several IVR World congresses, and for the meetings of the Societas Ethica. A very special mention is due to the W.A.Visser't Hooft consultations held at the Ecumenical Institute of Bossey (Switzerland) since 1993, centred on matters of concern for Christian social ethics (and the sustainable society in particular), in which I had the privilege to participate. These consultations reinforced my conviction that the churches can offer a meeting place for all those concerned with the defence and promotion of life. I had already experienced that in this country at the meetings of the MCKS (Social Centre for Church and Society).

Personal acknowledgments are due to Derk Rijpma, Lukas Meyer and Ko van der Wal for inspiring conversations and exchanges. Mme Parain-Vial (Paris) acted as an indispensable sounding-board. Lots of patience were asked from the familial environment of the author — a patience that is gratefully acknowledged. I also want to thank my son Willem for pressing me into the computer age.

I did not think it necessary to list my former (short) publications on the subject in the bibliography attached to the present book. Let me only mention, as the last and most extensive discussion preceding it, the article "L'avenir de la politique internationale de l'environnement *de lege ferenda*", published in the yearbook of Stratégies énergétiques, biosphère & société (SEBES) on *Le droit international face à l'éthique et à la politique de l'environnement*, Georg, Geneva 1996. The discussion in subsection 5.2.2 of my book (trust in the future as a primary good) follows the same lines as those I adopted in my contribution to a shortly forthcoming publication (by the same publishers) on the liberal neutrality thesis ("The good life as a public good").

CHAPTER 1

INTRODUCTION

Putting the economy on a sustainable course has become a dominant issue in contemporary politics. In this book, my aim is to contribute to a clarification of the moral reasons that require us to consider the environmental needs of future generations. I shall consider those reasons to belong to social ethics, and to form the moral backbone of a search for relevant legal concepts and instruments.

Environmental problems have different temporal attributes. Some of these problems already trouble us at present, or in the very short run; others will confront remote generations. The long-term aspect in fact is a frequent one. From its very beginning, concern for the environment has reflected a preoccupation with the interests of future generations. As for the concept of the sustainable economy, it naturally calls to mind an open-ended temporal horizon. Now, it is important to realize that in wanting to extend its reach into an indefinite future, social action is in effect breaking new ground. In caring for the remote consequences of our way of life, we are moving beyond the limits of society as we traditionally understand it. Political and legal philosophy have always explained human society through interactive patterns (cooperation, conflict, contract) that operate between people living together as contemporaries. With the golden rule, moral thought has always converged on reciprocity. Remote consequences did not have to be considered in the past, because human power had a limited scope. As Hans Jonas formulates it in his "Imperative of responsibility": "(the) effective range of action was small, the time span of foresight, goal-setting and accountability was short, control of circumstances limited"[1]. There certainly was a sense of intergenerational continuity (more than we can claim to have at present, in fact), but beyond the sphere of actions and attitudes already beneficial for one's near posterity (setting, so to speak, the ship on the right course), the future was governed by a Providence quite independent of human will. We now are capable of causing (and so responsible for preventing) harm in remote regions of time, beyond the sphere of actual or potential intercourse. We can witness a famine in Ethiopia

---

[1] Jonas 1984, 5.

on TV, we cannot do so with future catastrophes. There formerly was no need, as there is one at present, to consider how our descendants in the year 3000 can be protected against the radioactivity generated by nuclear waste.

So the issue I want to deal with typically concerns sacrifices that have to be made on behalf of purely potential persons. Of course, the longer term is best provided for in many cases by caring for the next day on a continuous basis. But the central case I consider in this book is one of direct confrontation with the ecological interests of temporally remote populations. As Brian Barry formulates it,

> "it is quite possible, when we turn to environmental issues, to find examples of actions now that will probably on balance be advantageous over the next generation and advantageous or neutral over the next after that, but then increasingly bad for later generations."[2]

It should not be inferred by contrast that ecological risk within a shorter time frame is always met adequately. The present negotiations concerning climate change show how difficult it is to agree to the sacrifices needed for meeting grave risks that may already materialize within the lifetime of presently living persons or at least of their proximate descendants. There is a quite general problem of being rational in relation to the future.

The temporal extension of the scope of human activity creates a challenge to the legal order. This challenge is being met in a growing measure by the development of environmental law, but I think there still is much work to be done in order to give to the long-term future its rightful place in the background theory and the conceptual apparatus of law. Legal systems must adjust to new conditions of responsibility.

Now it is in social ethics that we first have to gain more solid ground. For the first question is, what basic perspective we should adopt when seeking what is right in relation to the environmental interests of future people. The subject is no easy one. "It has never been usual, and it is certainly not easy, to think in terms of duration when considering issues of ethical and political theory. Paradox, or even absurdity, is never far beneath the surface."[3] The vast literature on obligations to future generations that has grown within the last two or three decades shows how strongly any discussion of the subject depends on the philosophical premises that have been chosen in the first place. Utilitarian, Rawlsian ("contractualist") or communitarian approaches compete

---

[2] Barry 1989, 193.

[3] Laslett & Fiskin 1992, 6.

with one another. I would like to suggest, contrariwise, that it is not this variety of academic opinion which lies at the core of the subject, but a pre-philosophical intuition of justice across time that is shared by us all and that is already influential in law and politics. In my view, it is that intuitive conception which academic discussion should take as its starting point.

For a consensus is clearly emerging in contemporary society that it would be contrary to justice to ignore the presumptive environmental interests of future generations (nobody, to my mind, does openly defend an "après moi le déluge"). Our moral convictions tell us that we must share the resources of the planet, which have shown themselves to be finite, with our descendants. There is an intuitive feeling that each generation must deliver the world to its successors in the condition in which it received the world from its parent generation. Each generation is thus both a beneficiary with a right to use the planet and a trustee with the obligation to care for it. Although they also have other connotations, the concepts of "sustainable development" or of the "sustainable economy" reflect this moral understanding. We feel we have no more rights on the resources of the earth than its future inhabitants. What ideas are capable of articulating this conviction and of clarifying its implications within the circle of contemporary social theory? Let me say in a few words how I want to answer that question in the present argument.

1.1 THE JUST BASIC STRUCTURE

The very concept of a just claim of future generations on the resources of the planet (and the same goes for the concept of the sustainable economy) lets one take from the start a moral point of view on human society as a whole. It is the present generation, as it is organized in contemporary society, that is subjected to moral judgment in its relations to the processional reality of future populations renewing themselves across time (I shall devote some remarks to the ambiguities that characterize the concept of "generation"). This is not to say that the actions of particular persons escape moral and/or legal liability in respect of long-term environmental harm. Nor does it mean that future generations possess some collective identity (I shall argue on the contrary that harm to future generations must be understood as harm to potential individuals). What it means is that one is adopting from the start a general perspective on right and wrong in the distribution of an essential good or complex of goods between presently living people and potential people, and that the realization of this global distributive intent cannot be imagined apart from the workings of society considered as a system for the right distribution of social goods. This collective character of our issue also derives from the circumstance that a satisfactory environment has preeminently the character of a public good, and usually requires group action for its preservation; the reasons why securing the general good depends on institutions which coordinate individual decisions are particularly applicable here[4].

So responsibility is taken first of all by the presently living in their collective capacity of members of society (i.e. of citizens). It is society as a whole that is called to account, in respect of a basic distributive issue that arises between its present and its future members. That issue must be dealt with by different though complementary social mechanisms and legal instruments. Taxation policies next to subsidies for the development of environmentally "clean" technologies; administrative regulation next to individual liability for environmentally disruptive behavior, based on provisions of criminal law or of the law of torts.

Now what this general perspective calls for on the level of background theory is the conception of a *just basic structure* of society covering justice between generations. One should be able to say that it is a part of the basic distributive pattern of society that its environmental resources be kept at a sustainable level. In considering justice to future generations to be the moral essence of conservation and so of environmental law, one does'nt just postulate a new policy directive that must compete with others. Justice cannot be satisfied half-way: "justice is the first virtue of social institutions, as truth is of systems of thought."[5] One chooses a normative perspective that claims to govern society as a whole and to exercise a regulative primacy. In other words: if we take seriously the generally shared aspiration towards more justice between generations, we must accept the institutional consequences of that aspiration, and admit that states should recognize, as an element of their constitutional set-up in the widest sense, the absolute precedence of environmental values insofar as the conservation of an adequate resource basis depends on asserting such a priority.

Therefore, the claim I am presenting here is that the consensus on justice between generations in the environmental field, once it is chosen as one's star-

---

[4] Cf. Rawls 1971, 266-270 on relevant aspects of the public good situation, e.g.the free-rider problem and the problem of externality.

[5] Rawls 1971, 3.

ting point, necessarily points towards a theory of justice like Rawls', which is centred on the idea of a just basic structure of society and so offers the conceptual resource one needs in order to clearly articulate the fundamental nature of a commitment to sustainability. Rawls'theory all the more enjoys a paradigmatic (though of course not infallible) position in our context since it takes account, itself, of relations between generations,

Rawls defends the general primacy of justice: laws and institutions no matter how efficient and well-arranged must be reformed or abolished if they are unjust[6]. The primary subject of justice is the basic structure of society, or more exactly,

> "the way in which the major social institutions distribute fundamental rights and duties and determine the division of advantages from social coopera-tion."[7]

With Rawls, this structure is governed by the following principles. The first one stipulates that each person is to have an equal right to the most extensive total system of equal basic liberties compatible with a similar system of liberty for all. The second one determines that social and economic inequalities are to be arranged so that they are both: (a) to the greatest benefit of the least advantaged, consistent with the just savings principle, and (b) attached to offices and positions open to all under conditions of fair equality and opportunity[8].

It is the "just savings principle" (discussed in my chapter 4) that gives an intergenerational dimension to this set of principles. (But since Rawls does not, or does rarely, consider the environment, I plan to examine with some care what his just savings principle can help us with in our present context of inquiry).

I shall discuss at a later stage the difficult point that Rawls concentrates on the basic structure as a closed background system and so does'nt deal (at least on the same demanding level of social justice) with the eventuality that one

---

[6] Rawls 1991, 3.

[7] Ibid., 7. See also Rawls 1993, 11 and 258 for definitions of the just basic structure. Lecture VII in Rawls 1993 is entirely devoted to "The basic structure as subject".

[8] I reproduce the final statement (Rawls 1971, 302) at the beginning of 4.3 hereunder. The first principle claims a lexical priority over the second principle, and the second principle a lexical priority over other social aims such as the principle of efficiency or that of maximizing the sum of advantages. "Lexical" priority means that one cannot proceed towards a following principle before having fully satisfied the principle to which that sort of priority has been granted.

may have to think in terms of a global world system, as is the case with important environmental issues[9].

The claim I am making here (that the whole discourse on justice between generations and the sustainable economy necessarily postulates a just basic structure of society) leads to the further claim that certain doctrinal positions in social and political theory such as the utilitarian or the libertarian one, that do not allow for the concept of a basic structure, do not provide us with the theoretical baggage we need in order to articulate and think through the full import of an important trend in contemporary social thought which has already begun to shape social and political reality: the submission of society to a test of intergenerational justice in respect of the demands it makes on the environment[10]. One must apply, to that issue, what Thomas Nagel says about the more classic concerns of social justice:

> "...with regard to income, wealth, social position, health, education, and per-
> haps other things, it is essential that the society should be regarded by its
> members as responsible for how things are, if different feasible policies and
> institutions would result in their being different. And if the society is respon-
> sible, they are responsible through it, for it is their agent."[11]

The Lockean view that the task of government is limited to preserving the conditions for individual moral relations leaves no room for such a wider sense of responsibility nor of course for its being articulated by the definition of a just basic structure[12].

Let me emphasize that the basic structure pretends by definition to a regulative priority. Consequently, it cannot tolerate — with respect to the conservation of an adequate resource basis to be kept equal across time — a point of view according to which environmental goals should be considered as policy goals that are amenable, as a matter of principle, to trade-offs against

---

[9] Rawls 1993, 272 note 9.

[10] Ibid., 260-265: utilitarianism and libertarianism (Nozick!) have no use for a basic structure. The conception of intergenerational equity as requiring a moral "two-tier" system (Page) is shared by Singer 1988, Norton 1989 ("preemptive constraints" must be placed on the pursuit of economic criteria for resource use; we must abandon the search for a unified scale of value by which to measure resource-use decisions affecting multiple generations), Page 1991 (we need a "two-tier" value theory). Cf.also van Hengel & Gremmen 1995.

[11] Nagel 1991, 99-100. Ibid., 201: "Any way in which the society arranges things, any system it enforces, from laissez-faire to socialism, represents a choice which must be justified in comparison with the other viable alternatives".

[12] Ibid., 101-102.

other social aims (although I am aware that different factors, to which I will shortly return, favour the frequent occurrence of such trade-offs on the level of practice). The basic idea is that we must share the earth with all other generations, and either we do share it or we don't: it is clear that there is no middle ground, although the question whether that sharing is being put at risk in a particular instance can be (and often is) an eminently disputable one. But contemporary developments nourish the hope that the international community may be ready to draw the line somewhere.

It might be objected that even when it has been affirmed on a basic level of social ethics, intergenerational justice still meets a serious challenge when decision-making is confronted with urgent needs of the present. We shall see that this is a hot issue on the world level (2.2). Can justice to future generations be bought with lack of respect for the conditions of survival of presently living people? I shall claim (4.3.2) that a dynamic conception of ethics must recognize the reality of certain subjective reasons (in our case, the immediate or proximate character of urgent needs). The conflict between those reasons and the objective, impersonal demands of the just basic structure cannot be solved on paper by a diktat of moral reason: it can only be solved by striving for a better state of the world (economic and political) which would permit moral harmony. But let me suggest in any case that it is important, for the purpose of the present argument, to keep apart the two following avenues: making room for urgent needs on the one hand, and attributing a general discretionary power to decision-makers to trade-off environmental values against other social aims, on the other. I don't see how the concept of justice to future generations can be given any substance unless one first rejects the last-mentioned possibility.

I do not want to end this introductory discussion of the just basic structure before making the following remark. No student of environmental affairs can fail to be struck by their complexity, by their frequently very debatable character, and by the uncertainties that affect the empirical knowledge their solution would require. So the postulate of a just basic structure (and especially of its regulative primacy) might seem to be a very theoretical proposition indeed, which is put forward on a high level of abstraction but which cannot really claim to determine substantive decision-making. Let me list some relevant factors. (a) Environmental foresight can often arguably be served by different basic policies. So an element of political choice may be expected to exist from the start. (b) The lack of sufficient knowledge concerning the relations between man and his environment (consider the debate on global warming!), as well as the impossibility of foreseeing social or technological change (and the effects of the latter), introduce an element of risk-taking which largely resists normative treatment (what is a "reasonable" risk?). (c) Last but not least, the basic goal (a just distribution of ecological resources over time) shows a regrettable ambiguity, for there is considerable leeway in defining the values which that aim wants us to secure in particular. What standards do we precisely have in mind?

Still other factors could be mentioned which combine to make the just basic structure a very indeterminate one, allowing considerable differences of opinion about its translation into concrete institutions and policies, and leaving (in actual fact) a lot of room for trade-offs between environmental values and other social interests. But let me now quote Rawls on indeterminacy.

> "The indeterminacy in the theory of justice is not in itself a defect. It is what we should expect. Justice as fairness will prove a worthwhile theory if it defines the range of justice more in accordance with our considered judgments than do existing theories, and if it singles out with greater sharpness the graver wrongs a society should avoid."[13]

The last-mentioned aspect (singling out the graver wrongs) can be related to the well-known observation that we know what is contrary to justice much better than we know what positively conforms with it. And do we lack such knowledge? The graver wrongs we can currently identify with some measure of probability surely give to the basic structure a chance to assert in practice its unqualified priority. Beyond that, I think one should not underestimate the power which the official recognition of a just basic structure can exercise as an argument in debates about the need for environmental action; it makes a difference whether one puts at risk the realization of a social aim amongst others, within a context of mutual trade-offs, or whether a plausible case can be made for the claim that fidelity to a fundamental commitment of the community is involved. It should be remarked, finally, that the relatively indeterminate character of the principle of intergenerational justice can be considered to subject us to the duty to seek a consensus on sharper definitions, be it as concerns the criteria of justice itself or its context of application.

---

[13] Rawls 1971, 201.

1.2 THE TWO PERSPECTIVES

I have claimed that in taking as one's starting point the now widely shared social aim of securing justice between generations in the environmental context, such as it inspires the search for sustainable policies, one is necessarily led towards asserting that there is a just basic structure of society, with its regulative primacy, of which that aim is an important element. The argument must then concentrate on analysing the concept of justice between generations: I shall try to show that Rawls' theory of justice helps that analysis in different ways.

However, I think that a reasonably realistic treatment of the subject calls for a broader view. The essential point here is that when we have the intuitive feeling that justice requires of us, the living generation, to share the environmental resources of the planet with its future inhabitants, the very sense of that intuition (the term "justice" reveals as much) is that we take a moral attitude, an attitude of detachment in respect of the present and its short-term interests, which aspires to impartiality as between the interests of persons that presently exist and the interests of potential persons, and that this attitude has to compete inevitably in our actual lives with the quite irrepressible experience of being ourselves positioned in time, within a present separating past and future, from the perspective of which future generations at first seem to be hidden in a sort of remote anonymity that prohibits emotional identification. When it comes to sacrificing short-term values, the most serious commitment to justice still has to conquer the "moral distance" (Glover) created by distance in time. Accordingly, one cannot rest content with an affirmation of the moral point of view: one also has to ask what background motives, if any, make us *interested* in the welfare of future generations, in such a way as to sustain in practice the choice and actual observance of that moral point of view.

It is true that a serious commitment to justice has a motivational force in its own right, or so I shall claim. As Brian Barry formulates it,

"the desire to be able to justify our conduct in an impartial way ... is an original principle in human nature"[14].

The rationalist will say that morality ("the call of duty") must show its force where sentiments cannot be relied upon. But how strong is its voice actually going to be? Normative validity does not entail psychological

---

[14] Barry 1989, 364.

strength. The commitment to justice implies that one tries to identify and articulate all motives that give to future generations a greater visibility.

The question is the following: when we say we want to share the earth with its future inhabitants, do these only figure in our minds as human beings in the abstract, whose life chances happen to depend on ourselves leaving to them an environment fit to live in, or would this overextend our moral powers and is some closer relation implied? I think that one is right to suspect that moral reason would mostly have a hard time if left completely on its own and that it therefore is important to explore the motives that make us accord a value to the welfare of potential people. Are future generations merely the objects of our moral sollicitude or do they also embody, so to speak, a substantive dimension of "things going on", as those human beings whom we, the living, want to carry on with life and with everything we consider to have value in our life? I shall adopt the working hypothesis that there is such a natural (though rather inarticulate) understanding of society as an on-going reality, which makes it easier to explain the step that carries the concept of justice beyond its normal context of people coexisting with one another. But I shall stress at the same time that there is no preestablished harmony between that world of "other" motives and the demands of moral reason. What value do we accord to the welfare (and more radically, to the existence!) of *very* remote people, living in the year 3000 or 30.000 for that matter? Does an implicit belief in the perpetuity of society and of civilized conditions of life have an existential significance for us, in our capacity of historical beings? Or does our awareness of historical change undermine any felt solidarity with future people?

What I have just been indicating is the outline of an argument putting justice between generations within the wider context of practical motivation. In doing so, I feel inspired by Thomas Nagel's treatment of ethics as involving two competing perspectives. In his "View from nowhere", he says that the most fundamental issue about morality (next to being the most fundamental issue about knowledge, freedom, the self, and the relation of mind to the physical world!)

> lies in reconciling "the perspective of a particular person inside the world with an objective view of that same world, the person and his viewpoint included. It is a problem that faces every creature with the impulse and the capacity to transcend its particular point of view and to conceive the world as a whole."[15]

---

[15] Nagel 1986, 3. Ibid, 138: "Objectivity is the central problem of ethics".

The "objectifying impulse", says Nagel, already lives in us; it competes with our subjective reasons. Our moral intuitions follow its lead. The central problem of ethics is

> "how the lives, interests, and welfare of others make claims on us and how these claims...are to be reconciled with the aim of living our own lives"[16].

The subject of duties to future generations typically shows such a bifurcation of our basic viewpoints on the world. As I see it, its complexity is due in large measure to this dual focus.

(i) Taking our cue from Nagel's dichotomy, we can first identify an objective, impartial point of view, where we stand back from our position in history as the presently living generation, with its in-built power over the ecological fate of future people, and where we look impartially at the sequence of generations, none of them appearing to have more rights on the planet than the others. We consider our position in time as a contingent one. Distance in time becomes an irrelevant factor; the objective viewpoint makes us *see* human beings in regions of time we never contemplate in daily life. What we see is a procession of human beings spread out in a colourless temporal medium (a neutral succession of instants) which their moral standing is indifferent to. We cannot find any reason why position in time (either our own position in the present, or distance in time in relation to that position) should be relevant to the claim of human beings on basic ecological resources. (I note that the moral status of human beings is not affected by distance in space; residence at the antipodes creates no difficulties (on the level of principle) for the recognition of one's basic rights.)

Let us realize the strongly counterfactual nature of such a moral attitude. What the moral point of view is dealing with in this particular context is the total dependence of future populations on our good will (I shall claim that our relations with future generations are characterized by such an imbalance that no concept is useful that does not recognize social asymmetry as a characteristic circumstance of justice). The main point of justice between generations is to denounce generational egoism as an abuse of power. We, the living, perceive future people as claimants under a universal norm of respect for human beings, wherever situated in space or time. The image of future people as human beings we are accountable to seems to be generated by the moral point of view itself.

---

[16] Ibid., 164.

(ii) Now I said that the detached, objective view inevitably competes with our experience of being positioned within the dimension of time, and its related awareness of temporal *distance*. Nagel's "particular perspective inside the world" here consists in our existential inability to step out of the living present. What makes his conception of ethics interesting is that he does'nt consider the detached position to be a self-evident conquest of the rational mind which can leave consideration of the personal, the particular, aside; as he sees it, in effect, it is not so much a position as a dynamic *effort* to overcome our subjective perspective on the world. It competes with that perspective; it accompanies it as an impulse to transcend it. But it is inherently unstable, because we cannot simply ignore that we belong to the living and so to a particular moment in time.

What we first see, when we consider that subjective point of view, is a strong bias in favour of short-term values, which devaluates prospective states of affairs in proportion to their temporal remoteness. "Time preference" (Rawls) competes with moral reason. If the detached perspective can aspire, in a general way, to overcome this attitude, this is less sure in those cases where urgent needs in the present concur with prospective future ones. We shall see that Nagel opens the door for subjective reasons, associated with one's particular point of view, which challenge the "hegemony of neutral reasons". He mentions for instance the special claims of "immediacy". So we may have here a real moral conflict on our hands.

Nagel's dichotomy between the objective and the subjective, the general and the particular, describes practical reason in a fundamentally conflictual way. There is a basic issue of reconciling personal life with the demands of moral impartiality. It should be noted however that in considering the view from the present as a mode of subjectivity in Nagel's sense, one inevitably puts a stronger accent on collective attitudes than Nagel does himself in his discussion of the subjective point of view (cf. for instance the dominance of short-term values in our political and economic life).

There is yet another difference with Nagel. Though it reflects, so to speak, mainstream reality, a negative characterization of the subjective, temporally positioned point of view (there *is* a very general bias towards short-term values) should be balanced, in our context, by attention to a set of more or less latent and poorly articulated values, which have the quite opposite effect of generating an interest in future (and possibly remote) states of affairs. The psychology of our attitudes towards the future is a complex one. There is an at least latent interest, rooted in our personal lives and in contemporary culture and ways of life, which *supports* the forward-looking attitude of justice towards future generations and so helps moral reason in its struggle against time preference. As Partridge formulates it:

> "well functioning human beings identify with, and seek to further, the well-being, preservation and endurance of communities, locations, causes, arti-facts, institutions, ideals and so on, that are outside the selves and that they hope will flourish beyond their lifetimes"[17]

What future generations then represent for us is more than a new field for the morally objectifying impulse, with its unlimited but abstract sort of concern, although that impulse certainly works in us too; what we are concerned with (in the first place, perhaps) when we want to secure equal opportunities for future generations, is to make room for our own experience of the good, by giving it a future it cannot do without. Future generations then represent the future as it enters into the present meaning of things.

So what we find here is a form of the "subjective" that does'nt agree with Nagel's conflictual description of practical reason. The detached view presses us to evaluate future states of affairs in an impartial manner; the subjective view paves the way by drawing future states of affairs within the circle of presently living concerns. But the conflictual description remains a basically valid one, since those future-oriented interests have to struggle against a strong and very general time preference and can only do so by being articulated more explicitly than is usually the case. Nor should one expect some preestablished harmony between those subjective interests and moral impartiality over time: the view from the present is always a view situated in history, whereas justice to future generations (this is true, at least, for the longer run) must find support in values which presumably transcend the limitations of our historical condition. Moreover, our commitments may have a strongly parochial character which does'nt agree sith the global scale of environmental issues; justice to future generations seeks help from universal values. So the affirmation of intergenerational justice must in the end have a sufficient confidence in the independent motivational power of moral reason. I shall return to these problems in the last chapter.

---

[17] Partridge 1981, 204.

CHAPTER 2

CLARIFYING THE ISSUE

2.1 NO GENERAL ACCOUNT OF RIGHTS AND DUTIES BETWEEN GENERATIONS

An important characteristic of our subject is that the environmental context is essential to it. The international developments referred to, and the moral intuition they reflect, have made justice to future generations a global issue because of the risk of long-term environmental damage, and it is those risks justice to future generations is meant to avoid or to minimize. So no general account of rights and duties between generations is aimed at by the present book. I suspect that no such account could be given. According to John Rawls, "(how) the burden of capital accumulation and of raising the standard of civilization and culture is to be shared between generations seems to admit of no definite answer"[18]. We shall see while discussing Rawls that his argument on justice, which deals with savings in a general way, does not aim at defining particular burdens: it merely requires their impartial determination as between one generation and another on the basis of relative levels of welfare. I think it is a weakness of utilitarian theory to suggest that our relations with future people can be conceived in terms of a global and positive point of view, i.e. the principle of maximizing happiness[19]. No definite or at least no publicly ratified conceptions seem to fix the measure of intergenerational beneficence (except, partly, in totalitarian societies striving for maximum industrial growth). The only thing that can be said in a general way is that most people would probably agree with the statement that the world should be left to our children in a better state than we have received it in. This is an important point, of course, but it hardly provides us with clear directives for common action; the prior and more precise issue surely is, to what duties of justice we are held in a particular context such as the environment. It is *within* that structural framework that

---

[18] Rawls 1971, 286.

[19] An utilitarian paradigm is defended for instance by Birnbacher 1988.

the search for maximum returns is a self-evident guideline for policy-making.

2.2 THE SUSTAINABLE ECONOMY

The search for responsible environmental policies has in recent years found a common focus in the concept of the sustainable economy or society. I shall not try to present a technical definition of the highly debated concept of sustainability[20]; it suffices to say for present purposes that it points at a relation between man and the environment that can be sustained over time; what interests me is the moral, forward-looking intention that inheres in the concept. The following remarks are made with that limited end in view.

The World Commission on Environment and Development (WCED), presided by Gro Harlem Brundtland, gave pride of place to "sustainable development" in its report *Our Common Future*, published in 1987 and endorsed by the General Assembly of the United Nations in its resolution 42/187 of 1987.

> "Sustainable development is development that meets the needs of the present without compromising the ability of future generations to meet their own needs."[21]

So the economy must be put on the right track: it must maintain its environmental capital (its resource basis) on a sufficient level.

The concept of the sustainable economy reflects a norm of distributive justice over time: it is a matter of justice not to compromise "the ability of future generations to meet their own needs". But before developing that argument, I need to mention two issues which one should keep in mind when equating the sustainable economy with justice across time. 1) The search for a sustainable state of the economy cannot be divorced in the present world from the effort to secure greater justice between nations (in short, between North and South). 2) Second, the question what it is that must be sustained is not beyond controversy: so much so indeed that the notion of sustainability seems to loose much of its independent force. This creates a challenge for the moral interpretation in terms of justice, as that interpretation strongly favours, for

---

[20] Cf.Achterberg 1994, 19-40.

[21] WCED 1987, 43. I cannot deal here with the well-known but controversial objection that development is inconsistent with the aim of reaching a sustainable state of the economy.

evident reasons, the adoption of ecological demands offering the maximum chances for consensus, clear definition, and validity over time.

I now elaborate on these two issues.

1) The WCED report itself declares that sustainable development

> "contains within it two key concepts: the concept of "needs", in particular the essential needs of the world's poor, to which overriding priority should be given; and the idea of limitations imposed by the state of technology and social organization on the environment's ability to meet present and future needs."[22]

Let us observe to start with that the WCED report manifestly considers the environment within a global perspective: this is made clear by its translation of "the needs of the present" into "the essential needs of the world's poor"; a distributive issue on the world level is postulated right away. I shall claim (cf.3.1.2) that such a perspective agrees with the easily holistic, transboundary character of environmental problems, and with the difficulty in keeping concern with future generations (at least in respect of larger time horizons) within the limits of concern for one's particular country. So the "sustainable economy" here is the sustainable world economy, and its intertemporal, forward-looking interpretation ("future needs"), which is directed at future generations on the planetary scale, has no exclusive claim on our attention. There is, at the same time, the inherent aim of reaching a more equitable distribution of welfare between the inhabitants of our present world. Indeed, no real progress can be conceived as concerns environmental world issues unless the necessary sacrifices are distributed in a more equitable fashion than present international relations allow for. The UN Rio Conference has been very clear on the subject.

The second point referred to in the WCED text I just quoted clarifies the notion of sustainable *development*, considered within the same global perspective. Environmental resources only exist for those who have the capacity to tap them (without exhausting them). So the state of technology and social organization is a crucial factor. It is clear that the sort of development this calls for must be understood in a very wide sense indeed. A more equal access cannot be had apart from greater international equality in very different sectors of the economy and of society in general.

---

[22] Ibid.

Let us note that in translating the concept of the sustainable economy in justice over time, one does'nt only run across the additional imperative of justice "between North and South", one also meets a difficult challenge that inheres in the temporal dimension of the concept itself: what is the right response when acute needs of the present collide with the manifest interests of future people? The WCED report suggests giving an "overriding priority" to the needs of the world's poor, which presumably may limit or even set aside the claims of intergenerational equity. By suggesting in its general definition of sustainable development (quoted above) that sustainable development *is* equivalent to harmony between the needs of the present and the needs of the future, the Brundtland formula steps beyond this danger zone. I shall claim (cf.4.3.2) that such a conflict between survival interests cannot be suppressed on paper and that moral harmony depends on working for a better state of the world. This brings us back to the concept of a sustainable economy: it must be considered an aim of the sustainable economy itself to reach a degree of welfare for all which is sufficient to render such a collision improbable. The concept has no real substance unless it is associated with distributive justice on a global scale.

This is the right place to observe, in addition, the evident importance of population numbers: a sustainable world economy cannot be conceived of without adequate population policies (sustainability requires controlling depletion, pollution and congestion!).

2) I now adress the question, *what* should be "sustained" across time. What "needs" does the sustainable economy respond to? No student of contemporary affairs can fail to be struck by the variety of the answers given to that question; in the end, one gets the impression that all socially desirable aims are compressed within the notion of sustainability (beyond the sphere of "environmental" factors in any straightforward sense of the term), with extreme ambiguity as an unavoidable result. I shall concentrate on the ecological core of the concept, which after all is its historically prior one, and on the judgments on quality of life called for by the conception of a future integrity of the environment.

Now, even within these more manageable limits, there is a variety of conceptions which affects the clear positioning of justice between generations, and which is interesting from a philosophical angle because it reflects the tension between a detached and a more situated standpoint. The contrast I am alluding to exists between a view of environmental resources which tends to see them in terms of entities (eco-systems, ecospace) which it is for experts to identify with the help of scientific knowledge, and a conception which insists on the relevance of political, social or cultural factors for determining what it is that we must sustain. Let me be clear: I don't mean to say that this is an "either ... or ...", people being asked to choose for the one or the other view; I rather think that one is dealing here with two concurrent aspects of a same reality, the relative importance of which may be understood in different ways.

The expert's approach finds an illustration in the search for clear health standards in regulating pollution, or in the contribution of biology to the determination of what measure of exploitation some natural resource can bear. Consider for instance the notion of sustainable yield, and take the North Seas fisheries. There is an identifiable natural resource; and the question is, how we can assure a sustainable yield of that resource (that is, a yield that can be held constant over the years) by establishing some maximum that the fishing in- dustry may be called upon to respect. The question, typically, is a scientific one. The "ecospace" definition of the environmental capital provides a clear conceptual framework for the scientific approach. It has been expertly summarized as follows[23]. The interaction between the economy and the environment must take place at a rate compatible with the need to maintain the capital base. Either the level of environmental capital must be maintained, of the reductions in it must be offset by equivalent increases in produced and human capital[24]. Since important aspects of the environmental capital itself cannot be replaced by either produced or human capital, the levels of material extraction and waste generation must remain within the range of environ- mental pressures that the ecosystems concerned can cope with, which may be called "ecospace". If an economy is to be sustainable, its metabolism must be within the ecospace, which may limit its scale. Uncontrolled economic growth risks carrying the economic process beyond the boundaries of the ecospace, but as the patterns of production and consumption and the state of science and technology develop with economic growth, the environmental pressure per product or unit of income also drops. This is called "dematerialization", and if the rate of dematerialization exceeds the rate of economic growth, the overall

---

[23] Opschoor 1996, 336.

[24] The issue of compensating future generations for an impairment of the environmental resource basis, for instance by means of an increased investment in scientific knowledge or technological know-how, is discussed by Barry 1991, 259-273. Cf. van Hengel & Gremmen 1995 for an overview of the debate in the Netherlands concerning the general economic and ecological aspects of the issue.

environmental pressure will go down and the economy will become less unsustainable. From an ecological perspective, then, either economic growth must be curbed or dematerialization processes accelerated.

It is clear that this conception hints at the possibility — and the final authority — of economic and ecological determinations, whatever their complexity.

Now I think it is correct to say that it is a feature of the concept of inter-generational justice to call ideally for such an objective, supra-historical definition of the environmental capital base, established by means offering the maximum chances for consensus and clear definition, and subjected to a norm of equality over time. What we feel today is that we must share the planet with our descendants on a basis of equality; the subject of that concern ("the planet") is a set of basic resources whose importance for human life is presumed to remain more or less identical over time and whose finite character requires a distributive discipline from one generation to the other. The concept of sharing the planet would become an empty one if no such projection were attempted, by reason of the mutability of human needs.

"If impersonal value is going to be admitted at all, it will naturally attach to liberty, general opportunities and the basic resources of life..."[25].

There is a wish to transcend historical particularities and to secure justice across time in respect of values that can be presumed to be common to all human beings.

Now let me deal shortly with the conception which insists on the relevance of variable political, social or cultural factors for determining what it is that we must sustain. But I don't do so before repating the warning that no sharp conflict is being suggested between divergent views, but rather a difference in the emphasis that is placed on the various aspects of a complex reality. The expert will not refuse to admit that non-scientific factors play an important role in environmental matters, and the politician (if I may risk the term) will accept that scientific knowledge defines, as far as it goes, a set of basic conditions of physical survival.

The non-scientific factors alluded to may be illustrated as follows.

(i) The uncertainties of science introduce an element of risk management that cannot be governed by rules that are ready to hand. What is a "reasonable risk"? What is to count as a "threat of serious or irreversible damage" within

---

[25] Nagel 1986, 171: cf.also 4.3.2 on environmental goods as primary goods.

the terms of the precautionary principle adopted at the UN Rio Conference (see 4.1)?

(ii) The definition of relevant environmental factors itself is partly subject to judgments of value. There is an ecospace impact of the environment on the economic process, but what exactly do we consider to belong to the latter? What welfare functions is it meant to satisfy? Does it for instance embrace aesthetic or recreational values? I suppose that such interests as "survival" interests (reflected i.a. by standards of protection against nuclear hazards or by minimum clean air or clean water requirements), or interests in avoiding a massive disruption of the economy by the depletion of energy resources, are beyond dispute. But apart from that, there may well be a wide margin for collective choice (for instance: what degree of pollution or of biological impoverishment of our natural surroundings are we *ready to accept* in order to avoid severe cut-backs in our present way of life?).

So what this second point suggests is that there is a latent division between ecological limits to be determined by experts and whose neglect affects needs that are shared by all across time, and a much more "political" area where the acknowledgment of ecologically motivated constraints on the economy depends on controversial or culture-dependent views concerning the sort of society we want. In that vein, Birnbacher (1988) distinguishes negative action (omission and prevention of life-threatening harm and irreversible loss, on the basis of extrapolated basic biological and psychological needs) from positive action (conservation and amelioration of resources within a particular cultural framework). Do we need forests, birds, etc.? Does the sustainable economy require care for aesthetic values? Justice finds an uncontested and transhistorical field of action in the first-named context; it is there that it is a part of the just basic structure and so tolerates no compromise; the second context opens ecological values to competition with others.

Van Hengel & Gremmen (1995) draw a distinction between long-term sustainability problems characterized by the risk of irreversible ecospace losses, and environmental issues without such a long-term aspect (problems in "quality of living") which may be subject to widely different judgments of value. According to them, it is the first-named area of resource management that calls for a conception of intergenerational justice.

Would it indeed be justified to adopt as a conceptual guideline a two-phased approach according to which the detached, scientific point of view is the relevant one to the longer view, while the "optional", culture-bound concerns are at home in a more limited time-frame of forecast and planning?

The question is, whether it is possible to overcome the contingency of our historical situation, in the way or in the measure suggested by that conceptual bifurcation. What I am alluding to is the plain circumstance that the very confrontation with the finite character of ecological resources which we witness today follows from the present state of our economy and technology. Environmental threats arise because we are "hitting the limit"; we are doing so because of present or presently foreseeable demands on the environment i.e. because of our present way of life; and what we consider to be self-evident when considering environmentally responsible policies, is to retain the acquisitions of modern civilization with corrections we want to keep as limited as we possibly can. Nobody suggests going back to the Middle Ages. Now one might say that nothing follows from this for the possibility of defining (and preventing) the long-term effects of our economy on those *basic* aspects of life I described as survival interests. It just is the case that we, the living, presently risk causing these long-term harms, and that we have the duty to prevent them. But things look different when one considers elements of the environmental resource basis that play an essential role less for "man in general" than for "man in contemporary culture". Should we desire for our descendants a return to the times of candlelight and horse-drawn vehicles, our prospects in the field of energy would be happier ones than many now feel them to be. We quite naturally consider a decent life to embrace facilities (take the emancipatory effects of the vacuum-cleaner or the washing machine, for example!) that cause, together, pressures on the environment carrying us far beyond the level of mere survival. Meyer makes the capital point that if we wish future people to pursue certain valuable activities and projects, material conditions must obtain in the future which will have to be at a level well above that of people who have basic resources at their disposal, but no margin for occupations beyond the satisfaction of their physical needs. For instance, one cannot imagine people trying to become good violonists if they have to search for food the whole day[26]. In the literature, one finds a broad consensus in favour of interpreting justice to future generations in terms of an equality of opportunities, the baseline being understood to consist self-evidently in *opportunities equivalent to ours*[27]. The standards of modern life (presumably: in the West) operate as the guiding norm.

---

[26] Meyer 1997, 144.

[27] Achterberg 1994, 191.

So one might say that it is difficult to contemplate a fully detached determination of long-term environmental needs, based solely on transhistorical standards developed in different departments of science. We take our way of life along with us: the way of life that causes us to walk the ecological brink in the first place — with that qualification of course that respect for ecological limits may force us to accept important corrections of present economic and technological trends. We shall see later on that this creates an important stimulus to the criticism of contemporary culture; the sustainable society cannot be defined in merely economic terms.

Again, could we easily set aside our contemporary views on the good life when contemplating the needs of remote generations? I doubt it. If a majority is convinced that a worthwhile life depends on being able to walk in parks and forests, must it anticipate a possible fading out of that conviction in the minds of posterity, and abandon the planting of trees? One wonders how a phased approach might be made to work in practice. This is not to deny that the greatest possible caution in basing ourselves upon presently dominant values is necessary when there is a threat of irreversible damage to the natural environment. Vanished species don't come back.

A NOTE ON QUALITY OF LIFE JUDGMENTS

It is an interesting exercise to compare judgments concerning the conditions of life of future generations with judgments about the prospective quality of life of severely handicapped newborns.

The latter issue has been extensively discussed in recent years[28]. Its distinctive character is due to the circumstance that the subjective first-person perspective, which quite naturally claims a privileged status in respect of the quality attributed to life, can be no factor in the context referred to. So one is forced to make room (in a measure which invites discussion) for judgments that transcend the level of individual want satisfaction in favour of shared beliefs regarding the good life — in short, beliefs one can argue about. The situation resists an account in subjectivist terms. But what shared quality of life criteria *can* one imagine in our pluralist times? A.Sen has proposed a subtle approach that consists in defining inherently valuable "functionings" of persons (for instance mobility, or communication with others), quality of life depending upon the "capability" to realize them and combine them in one's personal life; so freedom to achieve (freedom of choice) stands at the centre of

---

[28] I am indebted to van Willigenburg, 1996.

Sen's conception[29]. This, by the way, confirms the unavoidable influence of cultural paradigms on any conception of the quality of life[30].

If we now consider judgments on the quality of life of future generations, in relation to threats to the environment, it is clear that the objectivist point of view, based on shared values, must claim an even greater importance than in the matter of handicapped newborns. We miss again, for evident reasons, a first-person perspective. But no analogy can be found with that limited degree of individual differentiation which still exists in the former case: as concerns handicapped newborns, it still is judgment on the consequences of concrete handicaps of individuals that is being asked for (although such an estimate is admitted by everyone to be very difficult and uncertain). The effects of environmental handicaps tend to be looked at in a more global and collective way. The accent, I think, is on environmental integrity as a basic, all-purpose "primary good" (cf.4.3.2 hereunder), within the parameters defined (at least in part) by certain cultural preconceptions.

2.3 THE CHALLENGE TO THE LEGAL SYSTEM

In section 1.1, I claimed (in line with Rawls' theory of justice) that justice to future generations, the forward-looking normative core of the sustainable economy, belongs to the just basic structure of society. It is clear that the legal system and its operation as an effective rule of law is to be found at the centre of this basic structure: the legal system defines the constitutional framework, provides for a system of equal liberties, regulates the market, es-tablishes recognized forms of property etc. In Rawls' theory, all of these are important institutional channels for realizing the principles of justice. Now what can we say about the challenge to the legal system created by an explicit social postulate of securing justice between generations? Let me first say something about that explicit postulate itself.

IS JUSTICE BETWEEN GENERATIONS MERELY ASPIRATIONAL?

The recognition of that postulate can be observed first of all on the inter-national scene. Support for the duty of States to ensure that the natural heritage of mankind is used and conserved for the benefit of both present

---

[29] Cf.ibid., 263f: van Willigenburg discusses A.Sen, Capability and well-being, in M.Nussbaum, A.Sen, The quality of life, Oxford 1993, 30-53.

[30] Cf.Musschenga 1993.

and future generations is to be found in many international instruments[31]. A useful restatement of that duty is offered by Annexe I to the WCED Report "Our common future", which contains a "Summary of proposed legal principles for environmental protection and sustainable development adopted by the WCED experts group on environmental law"[32]. The first principle states that all human beings have the fundamental right to an environment adequate for their health and well-being. The second principle declares under the heading of "Inter-generational Equity" that

"States shall conserve and use the environment and natural resources for the benefit of present and future generations"[33].

Commenting on that principle, the WCED legal experts group observes that the 1972 UN Declaration on the Human Environment already declares that to defend and improve the human environment for present and future generations has become an imperative goal for mankind. As for the Rio Declaration on Environment and Development (United Nations Conference on Environment and Development, Rio de Janeiro, June 1992), its Principle 3 states that

"The right to development must be fulfilled so as to equitably meet developmental and environmental needs of present and future generations."

I need not insist on the fact that because such a principle has been affirmed so frequently, other less directly future-oriented formulations in legal instruments concerning the conservation of natural resources should be read with the same end in view. But this follows in the first place (at least *prima facie*) from the nature of the subject itself, as all measures we take to preserve our natural heritage naturally reflect the longer view.

The recognition of a duty of conservation for the benefit of future generations (a duty that mostly rests by the nature of the case on government or on public bodies) also finds a frequent expression on the national level. So it would seem that contemporary practice allows the observer to affirm the existence of a legal principle providing for the recognition, on a basis of equality, of the environmental interests of future generations. The repeated

---

[31] See for international treaties: Birnie & Boyle 1992, 211-212 and 448-450, or Sands 1995, 200. An overview is also provided by WCED (Experts group) 1987, 43-45.

[32] WCED 1987, 348-351. The summary is based on the more detailed legal formulations that are found in WCED (Experts group) 1987.

[33] WCED 1987, 348; to be found as article 2 in WCED (Experts group) 1987, 43.

affirmation of that postulate does not hang in the air, it is not merely rhetorical, for it formulates the inherent goal of an already wide-ranging practice of environmental conservation which finds expression in binding provisions of national and international law. It articulates the moral core of the search for a sustainable economy.

It is true that this postulate, in the form in which it is affirmed for instance by the Rio declaration, is described by several authors as having a merely "aspirational" character[34]. If this is meant as a description of *the status* of the principle, I don't agree; I suggest it now is a fully adult part of the law. The circumstance that environmental aims frequently suffer from contrary economic or social interests forms no argument for asserting the merely "aspirational" status of a duty in respect of future generations: the validity of a principle is no straightforward function of its degree of enforcement. Nor is its indeterminate character a hindrance to affirming that it already is a source of legal obligations (although this may call for a difficult process of fact-finding and argument). I already cited Rawls on the topic of indeterminacy. What he says about the general theory of justice can be applied (with some slight modification) to the principle of justice between generations: it is true that its application must often depend on controversial findings or decisions, but it is worthwhile if it defines the range of justice in accordance with our considered judgments and if it singles out with greater sharpness the graver wrongs a society should avoid. Moreover, the strength of the principle as an argument is evidently much greater if it is seen as an element of the just basic structure.

I already noted, as concerns the topic of indeterminacy, that the acceptance of a principle of justice to future generations entails the moral duty to participate in the search for a consensus on sharper definitions, be it concerning the criteria of justice itself or its conditions of application.

Now the term "aspirational" could be held to refer to something else: the operation of the principle of intergenerational equity *as a principle*. If we follow Dworkin's famous argument, principles (as distinguished from rules, which follow a régime of "yes or no" applicability) are aspirational in the sense of having a certain weight which must be balanced with the weight of

---

[34] Cf.for instance Birnie & Boyle 1992. The authors insist on several aspects of the principle's indeterminacy, but concede that international practice points to an "emerging concern" for the interests of future generations. I also note that the principles drafted by the WCED legal experts are entitled "proposed" legal principles (although the experts observe as concerns principle 2, quoted above, that it finds support in many international instruments: WCED (Experts group) 1987, 43-45).

competing principles. They aspire to maximize the field of a certain normative point of view while having to find a compromise with other values in doing so. In short, their binding character resides in their having to be taken into account. This agrees with a realistic philosophy of value, which doesn't easily conceive values having an absolute weight in relation to others. But the question is, whether it is right to place the principle requiring the equal treatment of future generations within that general category of aims that are amenable to mutual trade-offs. I don't think it is, but that conclusion would have to be accepted more generally than it is at present. Either justice to future generations is not taken seriously, or it is considered as a fundamental and non-tradable element of our legal systems, in the same sense as the basic liberties are generally conceived to be. Let us imagine a situation in which the legislature is confronted with a clear choice between the satisfaction of short-term economic interests and the avoidance of irreversible ecological damage. I don't see how the idea of intergenerational justice such as it has developed over the last decades can have the least reality if the second alternative is not given priority as a matter of constitutional principle (I use the word "constitutional" in a non-technical, functional way). This is what a recourse to Rawls' notion of the just basic structure is helpful for: it gives a firm profile to what one might call the moral constitution of society, thus letting us define priorities for its legal framework in a stricter sense. The principle of inter-generational equity ranks higher than the common run of principles we find in our legal systems.

NATIONAL/INTERNATIONAL

I claimed that the principle of securing justice to future generations in the environmental sphere on a basis of equality has found recognition both at the national and at the international level. This calls for some further comment, in order to clarify the use of the term "legal system" and to avoid ambiguities about the level on which the "just basic structure of society" is discussed.

It is evident, to start with, that the principle is a principle of international law. It finds explicit support in many international instruments, and it articulates the wider temporal horizon implicit in many forms of international cooperation on the environmental front. Its being part of international law responds to the frequently transnational scale of environmental problems, and to the choice of a global perspective on the sustainable economy, which lets compete, with that principle, a search for justice "between North and South".

Now, a traditional understanding of the principle as a principle of international law would be that in declaring that "States shall conserve and use the environment and natural resources for the benefit of present and future generations" (principle 2 on intergenerational equity proposed by the WCED legal experts), one exclusively envisages its application in areas beyond the limits of national jurisdiction or in a transboundary context. But that traditional understanding would be a too limited one. As is made clear by an authoritative comment on the WCED proposed legal principles, they apply also

"in the entirely domestic domain, and area which, according to traditional international law, is subject to the exclusive jurisdiction of States."[35]

The legal principles are meant to be applicable to all instances of the use of a natural resource or an environmental interference in any part of the world[36]. This agrees with the global approach chosen by the WCED report "Our common future".

I think this penetration into the domestic realm must be squarely accepted as a basic feature of the principle of securing intergenerational justice. It actually codifies, and subjects to a mutual obligation between States, the many commitments to environmental values expressed at the municipal level (e.g. in constitutional provisions), considered from their temporal aspect. The choice of a planetary perspective on sustainable development, the need to define the "sustainable society", first of all, in terms of a commitment of mankind to greater justice in the world (both between the living and in respect of future people) is incompatible with a partitioning of the world in national jurisdictions closed to mutual criticism and control.

Insofar, the analogy with the human rights context is a striking one. But it has its limits. We here must bring up the difficult issue of rights. Let me first set aside the particular difficulties associated with the notion of extending legal (enforceable) rights to the individuals making up future (potential) populations. I shall come back to that (cf.3.2.3). There is a first-line obstacle that is created by the circumstance that

---

[35] WCED (Experts group) 1987, Foreword by judge Nagendra Singh, p.xi-xii.

[36] Ibid.

"(it) cannot be said that the fundamental human right to an adequate environment already consitutes a well-established right under present international
law"[37]

The penetration in the domestic realm of an international obligation to
conserve the environment certainly joins, to the protection of the interests of
states *inter se* in maintaining or restoring an adequate environment, the
protection of those same interests as interests of all individual persons (and as
this obligation also exists for the benefit of future generations, the latter
protection also applies to future persons)[38]. But does this imply granting to
individuals an enforceable right to an adequate environment? The concept of
such a right is still very much in dispute[39]. Important factors to be considered
here are: the resistance of environmental goods to an individualizing point of
view, and the circumstance that securing an adequate environment, though it
may be a matter of taking issue with a particular action of the state by an
appeal to individual rights, mostly amounts to the "programmatic" duty of
government to adopt and follow through the required policies, through
legislative measures or otherwise.

However, I think that the "rights issue" cannot affect an argument
according to which the duty of states "to conserve and use the environment
and natural resources for the benefit of present and future generations", with
its necessary penetration into the domestic sphere, results from the municipal
point of view in a constitutional norm endowed with a regulative primacy.
This is the main point that arises under the heading of issues for the legal
system; the task which the principle of justice to future generations confronts
us with in the first place is to make room for it, with the required standing,
within our several national spheres. It at that level of "society" in the sense of
a full-grown social organization, which contrasts with a still rampant
international anarchy, that we have to look at first for a just "basic structure"
enforcing respect for the environmental interests of future people. Now this
should'nt imply any neglect of the international dimension. Some would say
that the need for a just basic structure arises first of all on the world level.
What we need with the greatest urgency, because of the planetary scale of the

---

[37] Ibid., p.40.

[38] Ibid.

[39] Cf.ibid.p.40-42 on the lack of direct support in international instruments or in provisons of
municipal law. One should distinguish, from that general issue, the competence of individuals to
present claims within the framework of specific municipal legislation.

problems we have to solve, is the creation of supranational institutions having the power to determine and enforce just distributions between countries and in regard to potential populations as well. I don't dispute that urgency (I think one should add to it the need for a wider appeal to the notion of the "common heritage of mankind"), but I think that a definition of the just basic structure involving concern for future generations should start at the level of social organization that still occupies the foreground in our present world, that still is the basic one from an operational point of view, and that has set the stage for the theory of justice till very recent times. It is there moreover that it is able to connect most directly with the concepts of the rule of law or of equal liberty.

ISSUES FOR THE LEGAL SYSTEM

What issues derive for our legal systems from the above analysis? A systematic treatment of the question, based on wide-ranging research in comparative law, would greatly overextend the present inquiry. So I limit myself to presenting a few topics for discussion.

1. Of course, there is no question of starting from zero; environmental law already offers a broad range of mechanisms for dealing with environmental problems having a long-term component (I am not entering here into the political or social reasons for its relative lack of effectiveness). The study of environmental law under a *lex ferenda* perspective means starting from an already complex body of law and looking there for indications of institutional and conceptual developments to come.

2. I mentioned, in my Introduction (1.1), the main components of Rawls' just basic structure, and I claimed that a principle stipulating justice to future generations (i.e. a broad commitment of society to keeping the resource base intact over time) should be considered to share in that structure's regulative primacy. There should be no trade-offs with considerations deriving from social aims exterior to the sphere of justice. As I see it, this generates the following issues.

(i) Granting an absolute priority to the interest of future generations in enjoying an intact environmental capital basis would involve a departure from the present situation of subjecting environmental interests to trade-offs with other social aims.

(ii) Commenting on lexical priority, Rawls observes that the concept of a serial order

"presupposes that the principles in the order be of a rather special kind. For example, unless the earlier principles have but a limited application and establish definite requirements which can be fulfilled, later principles will never come into play"[40].

The question is, in how far a constitutional commitment to intergenerational equity in the environmental sphere can answer to such a description (or rather: in how far such a commitment can be translated into a limited set of "higher law" ecological norms answering to such a description). Insofar as it cannot, what results for the principle of lexical priority?

(iii) Future generations of course are absent from the legal scene. But their interests should be entrusted to some form of representation at all levels of decision-making.

Those are the issues I now want to discuss in greater detail.

2.1. If I am right, there is no general practice, on the level of national legal systems, of endowing environmental values with a clear regulative primacy (as contrasted with a practice of declaring environmental protection to be an important aim of government). The question is, what follows for intergenerational equity.

Let me mention a 1972 US court decision which seems to show pretty well the general situation[41]. The plaintiffs had argued that their environmental interests were protected by the US Constitution and particularly by its 14th Amendment. The court says it cannot find in that text the decisional standards it needs to determine whether the plaintiff's hypothetical environmental rights have been infringed. Still more interesting for our purposes is that it considers the judicial process particularly ill-suited for solving problems of environmental control because

> "such problems frequently call for the delicate balancing of competing social interests, as well as the application of specialized expertise...Furthermore, the inevitable trade-off between economic and ecological values presents a subject matter which is inherently political..."[42].

---

[40] Rawls 1971, 43.

[41] Plater, Abrams & Goldfarb 1992, 357-360: Tanner et al.v.Armco Steel et al., US District Court, Southern District of Texas, 1972 (340 F.Supp.532).

[42] Cf.also ibid., 365 for Mary Ann Glendon's criticism of "rights talk". "A claimed right to clean air or water, or safe products or workplaces, makes little sense in light of the need for close assessment, in particular cases, of the advantages of greater environmental protection, or more safety, as compared with the (sometimes) accompanying disadvantages of higher prices, lower wages, less employment, and more poverty."

Now if it is the case that environmental values are, in general, held subject to such a régime of "inevitable trade-off", it is clear that the definition of an environmental resource basis to be maintained across time, and the acceptance of an unqualified constitutional duty to follow the policies this requires, must mark an important departure from that general practice.

2.2. I just cited Rawls on the conditions of lexical priority. I suppose the issue must be defined as follows (at the risk of suggesting a very simplified image of reality). You first have a general commitment to justice between generations in respect of the environment. You then have to specify this commitment in terms of a definite set of resources that have to be kept at satisfactory levels over time. You next have to define these levels and adopt the policies appropriate for reaching them. Now suppose that the prime instance you are thinking of when talking about lexical priority is the priority of the basic liberties (just as it is with Rawls, see 4.3.2 on primary goods and equal liberty). The question is, whether the protection of environmental interests does'nt basically answer to a model that is different in in the following important respect. The basic liberties "have but a limited application and establish definite requirements which can be fulfilled", whereas environmental conservation rather resembles a vast programme calling for a continuous process of implementation at all levels of government (of course, this broad characterization does'nt exclude the eventuality of grave menaces to the environment which call for urgent measures having nothing programme-like about them!). The question arises, how regulative primacy is to be secured for the values in question.

2.3. An interesting analysis of desirable legal developments was presented some years ago, on the basis of Swiss and German doctrine, by the Swiss constitutional lawyers Peter Saladin and Christoph Andreas Zenger. I think it clarifies the situation in several respects.

The starting-point of their argument is that when it provides in its constitution for the basic liberties of the person, the "Rechtsstaat" (government according to the rule of law) implicitly assigns to itself the task of guaranteeing those same freedoms to all future persons. For instance, when article 1 of the German constitution proclaims the intangible status of human dignity, no reason can be imagined why that provision should be held to be "zeit-spezifisch" i.e. why its application in respect of future states of affairs should be limited to a certain period of time[43]. But what is the use of saying

---

[43] Saladin & Zenger 1988, 63, 77.

this, since future people do not yet exist? Saladin and Zenger's answer is that the basic freedoms are no mere "Abwehrrechte" i.e. rights defining, so to speak, a legitimate defensive posture against the encroachments of state authorities: according to contemporary conceptions, they also define affirmative duties of the state, that is tasks which government must assume in order to give, to the basic freedoms, a genuine reality (so the basic freedoms are "Schutzrechte")[44]. So what they argue for is a direct inference of the welfare function of government from the basic freedoms (a function to which they don't consider it to be imperative to associate the notion of particular economic or social rights).

Now, as environmental harm is capable of destroying the physical conditions of liberty, it follows that government has the constitutional duty to care for the integrity of the environment within an indefinitely open time frame (I shall claim that the same conclusion can be argued for within the framework of Rawls' theory of justice: see 4.3.2). Saladin and Zenger also remark that the democratic principle of majority decision looses its legitimacy when the majority imposes on future generations an irreversible degradation of the environmental resource basis[45]. A similar argument is developed by Rawls: the conception of justice of a democrat includes a provision for the just claims of future generations[46]. Saladin & Zenger argue moreover that the irreversible reduction of the basis for future life options is undemocratic by itself: democracy is built upon the idea that the minority of today must be able to become the majority of tomorrow.

As they very convincingly draw the protection of the environmental interests of future generations *within the circle of existing constitutional commitments* to the protection of the basic freedoms, Saladin and Zenger strengthen the case for attributing, to a principle of environmental equity across time, a status excluding the discretionary power of goverment to decide trade-offs with other social aims[47].

---

[44] Ibid., 95f. Cf.for the notion of affirmative duties of government in US constitutional law: Laurence H.Tribe, American constitutional law, Index.

[45] Ibid., 32, 99.

[46] Rawls 1971, 296.

[47] Saladin & Zenger 1988, 105-106: they do make an exception for the urgent needs of presently living people which are incompatible with a full protection of future ecological interests; but this exception is limited to the respect of minimum conditions of human dignity (the living have a right to such respect as well).

2.4. The principle of intergenerational equity is specified by Saladin & Zenger in a draft declaration of the environmental rights of future generations. As I indicated already, what they are contemplating is a set of affirmative duties of the state; so their draft declaration does not pretend to formulate directly enforceable rights, it rather stipulates ecological aims (clean air, pure water etc.) which it is the duty of government to pursue as a matter of constitutional priority. It fixes the programme for a vast legislative, regulatory and judicial development of environmental law.

But as the stipulated rights are held to formulate preferred policies and not hard and fast, enforceable claims (they all point at a further process of detailed implementation), we again encounter the problem, how the priority of these policies over other ones is to be secured. The answer of Saladin & Zenger is to offer detailed proposals for the representation of environmental interests (present *and* future) at all levels of decision-making[48]. Specially appointed persons or bodies should be competent to argue for those interests, the constitutional status of the latter creating, in their favour, a burden of proof (i.e. decisions preferring competing interests having to show that none of the relevant environmental interests are at risk).

2.5. Because they do not think primarily in terms of enforceable rights, Saladin and Zenger are successful in evading technical objections against the notion of attributing "rights" (in the sense of legally protected and enforceable positions) to future people. No objection can be raised against the basic idea of representing the interests of potential people (see 3.2.3).

2.6. Rawls' comment that "a limited application", and the possibility of translating them into "definite requirements", must condition the grant of a lexically preferred status to certain values, exerts pressure in favour of a "hard core" or "baseline" definition of the resources constituting the environmental capital to be maintained across time.

I already mentioned views tending towards a distinction between a restricted definition of hard core ecological constraints whose neglect would presumably affect future generations independently of cultural change, and a broader range of environmental values, to be defended within a shorter prospective time-frame, that would be centred on present conceptions and ways of life, and open to trade-offs with other social aims. I expressed some doubts concerning this two-tiered approach (cf.also my chapter 6), but this is one of the many points on which I readily defer to further discussion.

---

[48] Cf.ibid., 109f

2.7. The above remarks are not meant to assert that a constitutional recognition of environmental quality as one of the fundamental aims of government (but with no clear regulative primacy) is useless for purposes of intergenerational justice. It allows one to insist that all branches of government consider long-term environmental values in a reasoned way, no matter what those branches ultimately conclude[49].

2.8 No obstacles should be placed to the recognition of the environmental interests of future persons within the law of torts, when environmental groups can point, on behalf of the latter, to a risk of long-term environmental damage[50].

3. I now mention an important conceptual issue that arises on the international level.

A very interesting concept has been introduced in environmental law by the 1982 UN Treaty on the Law of the Sea: the concept of the "common heritage of mankind"[51]. I shall not dwell on its technical aspects: it is the conceptual richness of the notion which I want to insist upon. Let me say first of all that it formalizes the global ("common") character of a particular resource or complex of resources, with derivative *erga omnes* obligations of all states. It is the very principle of state sovereignty that is is called in question; the concept logically calls for a common, supranational form of management of the resources placed under its jurisdiction. Next, and still more importantly for our purposes, what is affirmed is the existence of an "heritage of mankind": the resources in question have been received from our ancestors and they must be passed on to our posterity. So duties of good conservation are part and parcel

---

[49] In that sense: Krier, The Environment, the Constitution and the Coupling Fallacy, 32 Michigan Law Quadrangle Notes 35 (1988), cited in Plater, Abrams, Goldfarb 1992, 361-364. For instance, the Dutch Constitution, art.21, provides that the protection and improvement of the environment is a matter of governmental concern.

[50] Cf.for the Netherlands: Nieuwenhuis 1997, 135, mentioning the Hoge Raad decision "de Nieuwe Meer" (HR 27 juni 1986, NJ 1987, 743). The Hoge Raad decides that the environmental groups asking for an injunction are not required to specify what interest they have themselves in the case, nor what (other) interests are at stake (the interests of persons in the vicinity? the interest of all nature-loving people? etc.). The general interest in the integrity of the environment is considered to offer a sufficient basis for legal action. Nieuwenhuis argues that this "generalizing" of the concept of interest opens the door for considering the interests of future generations.

[51] Cf.Birnie & Boyle 1992, 120-121, 390-391 and 448-450 for a more detailed account and for treaties introducing related notions.

of the concept's significance. It is easy to see that its potential is due to this combination of a planetary scale with an intergenerational dimension: it is mankind itself, considered as a unity within space *and* as a continuous entity within time, which is the "owner" of the resource placed under the concept's jurisdiction. This may all sound rather utopian in view of the very limited chances that have been given as yet in international practice to the concept, but it surely agrees with the logics of the ecological situation we already are in at present.

I said that the concept of common heritage points the way towards transcending state sovereignty; it also has a clearly critical potential in respect of the environmentally negative aspects of contemporary society in general. The Belgian author François Ost (1985) has developed the idea that our main legal concepts (he particularly insists on the absolutist conception of property enshrined in the Napoleonic Civil Code) are indebted to what he calls "a logics of appropriation" which does'nt work, or has negative effects, in respect of the environment. Environmental conservation calls for a holistic, cross-boundary approach which also endows resources with an inalienable status across time. Ost finds an ancestry for the common heritage concept in all traditional configurations which ground the unity of a material whole (i.e. of a complex of goods) on the unity of the person, of the family, or of the group, thus securing its inalienability. The integrity of a resource is protected over time when it reflects the continuity of a social entity and secures its economic basis. There is a clear incompatibility with the structural tendency of capitalist markets to favour the mobility of goods.

Ost also finds a partial inspiration in contemporary legal structures such as usufruct or the common law trust.

As I have already been using US materials, let me use them still somewhat further by mentioning an interesting development in US environmental law which shows traits similar to those of the common heritage concept: the public trust doctrine. Although it is still unclear on many points, the doctrine (which has now been affirmed by the courts on different occasions) postulates "a duty of the state to protect the people's common heritage of streams, lakes etc., surrendering that right of protection only in rare cases when the abandonment of that right is consistent with the purposes of the trust..."[52]. In a stimulating

---

[52] National Audubon Society v.Superior Court (Mono Lake), Supreme Court of California, 1983 (33 Cal.3d 419, 189 Cal.Reptr.346, 658 P.2d 709), in Plater, Abrams and Goldfarb 1992, 388. The public trust doctrine is discussed by these authors on 365-412.

comment on the many questions raised by the doctrine, the authors of a casebook on US environmental law argue that if the beneficiaries are future citizens as well as present (and past) citizens, then it appears that a simple majority vote of a present-day legislature may not be enough to permit irrevocable diversion or alienation of trust resources[53]. In their commentary on the 1983 Mono Lake decision of the SC of California, they observe that the court

> "defined a public trust role for the state government that held it to a new and higher standard of decision-making. The state could no longer merely be a mechanism of majoritarian politics; it apparently now had enforceable long-term fiduciary obligations to an indefinite constituency including generations unborn."[54]

2.4 THE ECOLOGICAL DISCOURSE AND JUSTICE BETWEEN GENERATIONS

The lack of a respectful relation with our natural environment lies at the heart of our present problems. Our economic and technological development is reaching the limits of what the planet can bear. The resulting awareness of nature as a finite and fragile, and therefore precious entity, has generated a philosophical discourse which tends to react against man's destructive self-centredness by going to the other extreme of considering nature as an all-encompassing reality having an intrinsic value. The resulting challenge to our traditional conceptions is a healthy one; nonetheless, I think it is important to dissociate concern for future generations from that style of thought. I do not want to deny the reality or the worth of concern for the integrity of nature - nature experienced in its full otherness. But I think that when we want to clarify the intuition that we have duties towards future generations, it is a man-centred (anthropocentric) perspective that should have priority.

This is not the place to discuss in a philosophically serious fashion the question of intrinsic value. I can only say that I feel convinced by those who claim that any value rests, in the final analysis, on a human act of valuation (whether that value bears a clear relation to human well-being or not: it may

---

[53] Ibid., 376.
[54] Ibid., 391.

reflect an aesthetic admiration for the complexity of the natural world). Within our present context of discussion, the inevitably anthropocentric origin of value even gets a sharper profile. Concern with nature assumes a primarily instrumental function: we care for it in order to secure the ecological conditions of future human life. For it is human beings we are then dealing with, whom we perceive to be the victims of a particularly strong handicap: the issue, plainly, is one of social ethics, and it must be solved by an interpretation of the principles we are committed to in that particular field.

In a remarkably suggestive article, the French philosopher Chantal Delsol has suggested that contemporary ecological discourse *indirectly* but forcefully expresses a wish for social continuity which present-day modes of thought make it difficult to articulate explicitly[55]. Indeed, Delsol argues, why should we keep the stage in repair for a play without performers? To conceive of nature as a world we should preserve: this amounts to placing a bet on the future of Man ("parier sur la durée de l'homme"). There is a tacit but fundamental desire for keeping open the doors of history which contemporary modes of self-awareness hinder from expressing itself, because they glorify instantaneous gratification ("une éthique de la complaisance") and so cannot recognize that the creation and realization of values extends across time ("un bien inscrit dans la durée")[56]. Delsol mentions, on the level of daily life, building up a career, developing a friendship, caring for some artistic or scientific achievement. We should reflect upon our concern with the long-term future in similar terms.

But it is noteworthy that Delsol excepts "deep ecology" ("écologie profonde"), as distinguished from more pragmatic ideas on conservation ("environnementalisme"), from that interpretation. Deep ecology, as she sees it, seeks immortality through a fusion with Nature, understood in a manner close to pantheism. The death of society, tacitly accepted (though possibly not rejoiced in?) as an eventuality, is compensated for by endowing nature with a sacred character.

I don't need to repeat that the present argument works on quite different assumptions.

---

[55] Delsol 1994.

[56] Cf.5.2.1 hereunder for the strongly convergent views of John O'Neill.

2.5 MACRO-ETHICS

I already remarked on the dimensional issue: the question of respect for the interests of future generations can arise at different levels (local, national, or global). Because of several convergent reasons, I then singled out the level of society (which mostly coincides, within the contemporary world, with the national level). It is on that level that action has to be coordinated within the normative framework of the just basic structure. How we must respond, from that level onwards, to the frequently global nature of environmental issues, is one of the main challenges for contemporary world politics.

Now it is worthwhile to pause a moment in order to become aware, behind the field governed by the theory of justice (and the study of its political context), of certain background questions of general ethics that also arise in connection with the scale of the ecological predicament. It is for these questions that I suggest the term of "macro-ethics". What they indicate is that *in taking a moral point of view at all* in respect of environmental damage over time, we constitute ourselves moral agents on a level of responsibility that largely escapes traditional categories.

The dimensional aspect already makes itself felt when we ask how our shared responsibility for organizing intergenerational justice connects with the moral responsibility we traditionally ascribe to the individual person exclusively. But this is an issue that also arises in many other contexts and so I let it rest[57].

What I rather have in view in speaking about macro-ethics is that a commitment to justice between generations makes us assume responsibility for the consequences of our contemporary way of life. It is in the end our whole economy on which a moral judgement is passed. One could imagine a society like ours, but so mentally subservient to its own creations (the "iron" forces of the market, the "autonomous" dynamics of technological develop-ment) that it would regret the environmental misfortunes of future people caused by its way of life, but see no way for doing something about them (except returning to the Middle Ages). By denying its power to act, it would have avoided taking a moral position at all. One wonders in how far such a denial doesn't implicitly govern attitudes in our own society.

---

[57] Cf.Rawls 1971, 114f on principles for individuals in connection with the principles of justice, which govern institutions.- Of course, the one level does'nt *exclude* the other: we feel we have a duty together (a duty that must lead to action on the public level) to prevent or sanction ecologically irresponsible behavior by individuals.

Now if we collectively assume responsibility for the negative consequences of our way of life, to whom to we owe it? At first sight, the question finds an easy answer. We owe it to future generations, as a matter of justice. Future generations have an equal right on the finite resources of the planet. Considering the frequent rightness of defining the issue in such global terms, I think it would be appropriate to say that "we", the living generation, constitute ourselves as one collective moral agent in respect of relations across time; in accepting the norm of justice between generations, we bet on our capacity to organize ourselves as one moral agent on the required level of preventive action.

But that responsibility has an even more radical side to it. When we think about justice to future generations, we need not have in mind a risk to the survival of Man, nor even to the continuity of civilization: contemplating the risk of ecological decline is enough. We then desire a just distribution of ecological resources over time against a mental background of self-evident continuity: things shall naturally go on, but they should do so in the right way. However, we all know today that the risks to the environment carry, potentially, a risk of catastrophe. Does justice require of us that we avert it?

I think one should start here by declaring justice to be incompetent. Justice dictates the just treatment of future people, it does'nt demand that *there be* future people. One cannot derive from it the imperative that humanity must survive. The human beings between which the virtue of justice wants to shape right relations are presumed to come on the scene.

But there is a sense in which the motivation for respecting justice in our relations with future generations is related to awareness on our part of the more radical sort of risk. For it is easy to see that justice also is an *instrument* for the overriding goal of collective survival or minimum social continuity. By conceding to future generations equal rights on the finite resources of the planet, and by organizing a correspondingly "sustainable" state of affairs, we prevent an ecologically induced breakdown. So in respect of actual motives, justice between generations does not only respond to an obligation of justice *in se*, it also serves to avert a risk of catastrophe we feel to lurk in the background. Consequently, the question is a relevant one whether the goal of survival is itself capable of being argued for, and if so in what terms.

My position in chapter 5 shall be that we are not dealing here, in the first place, with a normative issue ("should humanity survive?"), but with an aspect of the *meaning of life*. An implicit trust in the perpetuity of man's presence on earth (in better circumstances than a life that is "nasty, brutish and short") conditions many aspects of what makes life worth living. So when we work for justice between generations, that trust can be qualified as an important aspect of what justice itself is about. Adequate environmental resources condition the future existence of a decent standard of living; securing such future resources serves the existential need of present and future people for confidence in "things going on". Because of its importance for our lives, that confidence must be considered to be an object of just distribution (a "primary good") in its own right, which also determines the worth of liberty. Accordingly, if justice does'nt demand that there "be" future generations, it still requires us to do everything we can in order to avert the prospect of catastrophe (this practically amounts to the same thing).

The conclusion I just arrived to depends on accepting the premise that trust in the perpetuation of human affairs is indeed a widely shared condition of a life worth living. It then becomes a part of what we owe to one another as human beings to do our best to help humanity survive.

An entirely different avenue consists in affirming on metaphysical grounds that humanity has the duty to care for its perpetuation. On that ultimate level of macro-ethics, the most interesting contribution has been offered by Hans Jonas in "The imperative of responsibility" (1984), originally published in Germany in 1979. Jonas develops a squarely metaphysical argument about the supreme value of perpetuating mankind, towards which I will turn in chapter 5. That argument is highly controversial; to my mind, its introduction, which consists in a compact description of the altered nature of human action and of principles and method in future-oriented ethics, is much less so. It puts the macro-ethical dimension in perspective but is already relevant in many respects on the less metaphysical level of arguing for justice between generations. Let me mention its principal points[58].

Jonas starts with the proposition that in our search for an ethics of responsibility for distant contingencies, it is an anticipated threat to the image of man that helps us to detect, indirectly, our normative conception of humanity. The perception of evil is infinitely easier than the perception of the *bonum*; "it is more direct, more compelling, less given to differences of opinion or taste". Of the good we become sure only via the experience of its opposite. Now, where few analogies in past or present experience (or none at all) exist for possible evils, the "creative imagination" must take over; such an anticipation becomes itself the first duty of ethics. We must visualize the long-

---

[58] I summarize Jonas 1984, 25-34.

range effects of technology, and summon up the appropriate feelings of fear (Jonas here suggests a sort of moral education of our emotional dispositions). But, says Jonas, the uncertainty of our extrapolations threatens to render that insight ineffectual; when sacrifices are asked for on behalf of alleged distant effects, uncertainty easily serves as an alibi for inaction. So uncertainty has itself to be included in ethical theory, and made the object of a new principle: "the prophecy of doom is to be given greater heed than the prophecy of bliss." When the stakes are raised and when irreversible damage to the biosphere is a possibility, we must "bow to the command of caution". This surely applies when there is a risk of infinite loss (the survival of man) against chances of finite gains. Jonas counters the reproach of "pessimism" by remarking

> "that the greater pessimism is on the side of those who consider the given to be so bad or worthless that every gamble for its possible improvement is defensible."

CHAPTER 3

THE SETTING

I now want to sketch in a few words how the nature of environmental problems and the conceptual features of our relationship with future generations determine the general character of the issue we are dealing with.

3.1. THE ENVIRONMENT: GENERAL FEATURES.

The environment (the word itself carries the implication) is an inherently collective set of life conditions, whose disruption tends to affect a more or less important number of people. Environmental damage typically concerns shared interests such as an interest in clean air, clean water etc. A sane environment is a public good. The same holistic nature tends to characterize the origin of environmental damage. Pollution is typically caused by the cumulative effects of human enterprise (a frequent instance is the pollution of rivers). Causation may lie with whole branches of industry or with habits shared by us all (e.g. the automobile); insofar, it bears few relationships (or none) to traditional ideas of personal responsibility. The current global warming negotiations provide an example of responsibility being shared between nations on the basis of relative industrial power. If environmental problems can of course exist on a local or short-term level, issues such as the diminution of the ozone layer, the greenhouse effect, long-term radioactivity generated by nuclear waste or the dramatic reduction of biodiversity, show how ecological phenomena can have an impact, in spatial or temporal terms, that has never existed before in man's relation with nature. The impact moreover threatens in many cases to be an irreversible one. To complicate matters even further, its actual occurrence or incidence is often surrounded with uncertainty. In short, it is all our traditional frameworks of moral or legal imputation (be it in the private or in the public sphere) that become suspect in this new domain.

The holistic nature of environmental phenomena calls for a non-individualistic perspective from the start. Preventive or corrective action has a predominantly collective character. Even at the grassroots level, action is typically taken on behalf of the grouped interests of many persons, or by environmental groups carrying out a general mandate of environmental protection within their country or even internationally. There is a predominant interest in influencing the legislator, the administrative regulator or the development of judge-made law. The problems that have to be faced require in many cases that action be sought for from government, and even there, no results can often be expected without international cooperation.

These holistic features are even more noticeable when one considers the long-term. The people living on some particular territory (a city, a region, a country) can perhaps be predicted in many cases to be the particular beneficiaries of an environmental policy, but there is a strong pull in the opposite direction (let us recall the Tsjernobil catastrophe: what populations should we consider to be the neighbours of a nuclear plant?). Industrial pollution in the UK and the US Midwest causes acid rain damage in Sweden and Canada respectively. The ozone layer and global warming issues concern the world atmosphere as a whole (the atmosphere is a "world commons"). Though we may intend to protect our own future nationals by taking measures against those dangers, this can only be accomplished by participating in global programs which in effect are directed at the future world population as a whole. The further we stretch our time horizon, the more this global spread of environmental disruption is likely to occur[59].

3.2 CONCEPTUAL ISSUES

3.2.1 What do we mean by future generations?

The concept of future generations shapes, by itself, very particular conditions for moral argument.

Problems of definition confront us at the very start. What do we mean by a "generation"? The Concise Oxford Dictionary offers the following choice. We can either mean a single step in descent within a particular family, or a whole body of persons born about the same time. It is clear that in the context of our present discussion, the second meaning is the more relevant one. But the words "born about the same time" show that a characteristic vagueness is present from the start. Let us look at demographic realities. No well-defined

---

[59] Brown Weiss 1988, 27: "Thus our concern for our own country must, as we extend our concerns into larger time horizons...focus on protecting the planetary quality of our ... environment."

entity corresponds to the concept of generation, used in the more group-like way I just preferred. Populations constantly renew themselves as some people are born and others die. Within a family, children follow their parents: no similar clear substitution occurs on the level of a whole community. When does a new generation begin? The more natural perspective is one of unbroken continuity; within any short period of time, the number of births and deaths is very small as compared with the group's total size. At any particular moment, those who already belonged to the group a short moment ago constitute an overwhelming majority. This explains the preservation of the group's identity over time: one has to wait quite a number of years in order to observe a total change in composition.

Laslett and Fishkin propose the metaphor of a procession, that is, of an irregular moving assembly such as "the Saint Patrick's Day Parade in New York City", where those "behind" us wait their turn to parade under the spotlight of the present[60]. What that image does is to show quite vividly that no bounded groups can be made concrete enough for the purposes of analysis. So particular generations (some writers prefer the term "cohorts") only exist by virtue of arbitrary stipulations on our part. For instance, generation X groups all people born between the years y and z. This, however, does not set apart a stable set of individuals: the "cohort" one has defined is a perpetually diminishing one. Let us take for instance our own position in time. "Our" position: that expression "denotes the immediately surrounding part of the procession, an indefinite area, but one within which both action and reaction can take place ... ".

> "We are conscious...of how irregular and indefinite is the boundary that separates (that) area from the remainder of the procession, fore and aft"[61].

In other words, the processional metaphor makes clear that the concept of future generations is a largely undifferentiated and open-ended one: what we are thinking of is one continuous flow, the end of which lies beyond our horizon. So the concept does not denote a structured whole, nor certainly an organism with a common will or common faculties for action. What we can expect is at the most a common fate.

It rather is the procession itself that forms a structured whole. There is an unbroken continuity: we do not merely see people following one another

---

[60] Laslett & Fishkin 1992, 11-14.

[61] Ibid., 12.

across time in some haphazard fashion. There is a gradual replacement of the individuals composing the family, the group, the nation, or mankind at large. We may speak of course about clashes between generations, but we do so against a background of continued identity.

Laslett and Fishkin observe that according to the processional concept they propose, justice over time

> "would...always have to be construed as justice between individuals past, present and future individuals — the titles "generations", "age groups" and "cohorts" serving only as indefinite indicators of those in similar temporal positions"[62].

It may perhaps seem a paradox that the facelessness, the anonymity of future persons (which I shall insist on presently), does not rob them of individuality. However, this individuality must not be understood in the sense of a full personal identity, but, less strictly, in the sense of individual places, individual (but average) life chances determined by the resources available at a certain moment for a certain number of people. The question of numbers therefore is a vital one.

Now there is one other structural point of view on relations over time which is quite different from the processional model because it does'nt conceive a flow of individuals, but hides individuals behind a screen: what I mean is the idea of a deathless institution or collectivity, which hardens identity over time into a stable form. That mental picture leaves no room for the distributive issue that is at the heart of the sustainable economy. But it certainly plays an important role within the context of identifying with potential people.

The ambiguities which are highlighted by the processional metaphor must inevitably colour the present argument. I trust that a central meaning of the term "future generations" is meaning is made clear in every instance by the particular context. In chapter 4, the emphasis is on remoteness in time, in chapter 5, on a future beyond one's own expected span of life. But this should not obscure the fact that generational egoism can already work at a shorter range — the elder people compromising the future of the younger.

---

[62] Ibid., 14. I have skipped Laslett and Fishkin's discussion of how kinship analogies cannot remedy the arbitrary character of the "cohort": see ibid. 8-10.

3.2.2 Anonimity and the limitations of the chain of love

It is important to realize the "moral distance" (Glover) that separates us from future generations, once we look further ahead than our own children or grand-children.

It is true that values we expect them to share with us can partly overcome that moral distance and even make us depend on them in a special way (cf.chapter 5), but I think the feature of distance in time and all it implies in the way of one-sided power relations and basic anonimity of future people should be emphasized first, as a sort of permanent background structure.

We don'tknow anything about the living conditions of future people nor about the values they shall wish to defend. We can only consider it very probable that certain biological base-line conditions that hold for us shall also hold for them. Let us also be fully aware of the fact that their life chances completely depend on our good will; we can despoil the earth without having to fear anything worse than losing our future moral reputation (nor can we of course expect an equivalent when doing something for their benefit).

Their strictly potential nature excludes any direct contact. There is no possible intercourse. We, the living, can leave good or bad things to them (either time bombs or a safe environment): that is the only way we meet (and a very one-sided one at that). Indeed, most people would claim that the most striking aspect of our "relations" with future generations is the absence of any form of communication. They would consider it to be a regrettable circumstance that modern humanity is capable of causing harm in these remote regions of time, beyond the sphere of actual or potential intercourse. Are we moving, in a sense, beyond the limits of society?

When we say that no communication is possible with future people, the context of our utterance plainly is the social one of actual or potential reciprocity. We cannot communicate with them in the sense of exchanging informations, opinions, material goods or services...or blows. Our activities can have the greatest possible impact on their living conditions, but we are comfortably freed from the pain of having to listen to their protest! So the only sort of influence they can have on our behavior clearly flows through moral channels from the start: it is a rule of self-restraint which makes us recognize future people as equal moral subjects and take account of their presumed interests. Nothing forces us to do so except the moral discipline we impose upon our unlimited power. It is by virtue of that moral discipline that the harm we cause to future people has the connotation of an injury we should avoid.

Potential existence makes for a strong sort of anonymity, which emphasizes the public, collective aspect of long-term ecological concern. It is true that we can try to explain that concern in the vocabulary of private loves. Must we not imagine a "chain of love", reaching into the future by every new generation's concern for its own direct descendants, such links being presumed to be sufficiently common and persistent to lend continuity to a civilization?[63]

Let me anticipate somewhat and mention here Rawls' motivational appendage to the circumstances of justice: the motivational assumption (see 4.3.1). Rawls assumes that relations between generations can find their motivational basis in parental care being repeated from one generation to the next. This is a very natural way of looking at relations between generations, but the problem is that it does not help us very much when we consider the full temporal extent of our destructive powers. It is typical of the environmental context that the present generation, if it is to act in a responsible way, may have to consider directly the interests of people in the distant future (let me mention the well-known instance of radioactive waste). Now, one could argue that the concept of the chain of love has the capacity to bridge that greater distance: let us simply anticipate and make ours, in our own minds, the love of our grandchildren for their grandchildren, etc. Such a psychological identification with future parental concerns certainly is a natural one in its very first phase. But it loses its plausibility when we look further into the future. Our children and grandchildren we can live with as individuals with a name, and so we can share their concern in an immediate way. Our more remote descendants are hidden in a complete anonymity.

Genealogical realities point in the same direction. They confirm that the parental, personal approach quickly loses its relevance when we look further ahead. A recent treatment of the subject explains this as follows.

("Your) great-great-grandchild will also be the great-great-grandchild of fifteen other people in the current generation, many of their identities now unknown. Presumably your great-great grandchild's well-being will be as much an inheritance from each of these fifteen others as from yourself. Therefore it does not make sense for you to worry too much about your particular descendant...". The authors conclude that "(the) further in the future is the hypothetical descendant, the greater the number of co-progenitors in the present gene-

---

[63] The "chain of love" concept is developed by Passmore 1974, 88-89.

ration, and consequently the more in the nature of a public good is any provision made for the future."[64]

Let us not forget, in that connection, that parental concerns are joined from the start by a public interest, the interest in education, and that when they decide to have children, people mostly trust in society offering to their offspring a certain spectrum of opportunities. So the "chain of love" concept reflects a too narrow perception from the very beginning.

3.2.3 Can potential people have rights?

I accept as a premise for the present argument that the modern vocabulary of rights

> "is a many-faceted instrument for reporting and asserting the requirements or other implications of a relationship of justice from the point of view of the person(s) who benefit(s) from that relationship."[65]

The question is, whether that instrument can be used in our case: does it make sense to speak of the rights of unborn generations against us?

It is clear that the idea of granting *legal* rights to future generations (in the full sense of claims that can be made effective in courts of law) presents specific difficulties of a conceptual and operational kind, whatever the strength of the case for justice may be. I already commented summarily on that issue. I don't think it is an essential one: the chances of the long-term within our legal systems do not depend on it. What those chances depend upon is the recognition of a legal *duty* shared by governments but also by individuals in responsible positions, which does'nt hinge on a prior grant of legal rights (that would be putting the cart before the horse). We can do with a corresponding attribution of *moral* rights. This of course is the conceptual minimum, for a relationship of justice would seem to involve, in every case, beneficiaries with a moral claim on its respect, even if its enforcement is secured without postulating rights in the legal sense.

Now there seems to be no difficulty in talking about the rights of future generations, in the sense of moral claims that have to be recognized by us, the living. We know what we are talking about; the heart of the matter lies in establishing that we have a duty of justice. However, there is one conceptual problem that can already be raised on that general level, and which threatens

---

[64] Daly & Cobb 1989, 39.
[65] Finnis 1980, 205.

our very acceptance of future generations as members of the moral community. Can beings which presently have a merely potential nature be the present beneficiaries of a relationship of justice? Can they be holders of moral rights to be respected by us?

A positive answer has been argued for in a convincing way by Joel Feinberg[66]. Feinberg develops the idea that the sort of beings who can have rights are those who have (or can have) interests. The concept of an interest is defined by Feinberg as: having the capacity to be the beneficiary of a right in one's own person, because one has a good of one's own. Mere things have no interests, because they have no good of their own i.e. no conative life[67]. Rocks have no interests, nor do plants, but animals have, according to Feinberg. Now the conceptual issue in respect of future people of course is'nt whether human beings have interests, it is whether interests can exert a claim upon us even before their possessors actually come into being. Our legal systems say yes:

> "the rights our law confers on the unborn child...are for the most part place-holders or reservations for the rights he shall inherit when he comes a full-fledged interested being. The law protects a potential interest...The unborn's child right to property, for example, is a legal protection offered now to his future interest, contingent upon his birth.."[68].

So the unborn child has rights which can be claimed by proxies on his behalf. Why then deny that same sort of protection to the human beings of the future? Potentiality, says Feinberg, is not the real difficulty. Unborn generations are more remotely potential than fetuses in terms of temporal distance and intermediate causal events, "but our collective posterity is just as certain to come into existence "in the normal course of events" as is any given fetus now in its mother's womb."[69]

---

[66] Feinberg 1980. I note that Feinberg's argument, as it is based on examples taken from the legal system (representation of future interests), addresses a possible objection to the recognition of *legal* rights. But the argument is fully applicable, to start with, to what may be an objection to the notion of *moral* rights.

[67] Ibid., 165: "no conscious wishes, desires and hopes; or urges and impulses; or unconscious drives, aims and goals; or latent tendencies, direction of growth, and natural fulfillments".

[68] Ibid., 178-179. "Contingent upon his birth": i.e. effective in the present, but in anticipation of birth actually occurring, and so voidable if he dies first.

[69] Ibid., 181.

The real difficulty rather lies in our descendants's anonimity, their present "facelessness and namelessness". But, says Feinberg,

> "they will have interests that we can affect, for better or worse, right now. That much we can and do know about them. The identity of the owners of these interests is now necessarily obscure, but the fact of their interest-ownership is crystal clear, and that is all that is necessary to certify the coherence of present talk about their rights."[70]

3.2.4 The so-called non-identity problem

Derek Parfit has raised the following conceptual issue[71]. Environmental policies can be expected to have wide-ranging effects within society. For instance, policies in the field of energy are likely to have an impact on patterns of domestic life or on travel facilities. So it is no wild flight of imagination to assume that those policies will also be influential in shaping the circumstances surrounding conception. The consequence is that policies in the field of energy are a possible causal factor in determining what individuals (with what genetic traits, and possibly: with what parents, in what situation) are going to be born.

Now Parfit's argument continues as follows. Imagine contemporary society to have chosen a badly inadequate policy which leaves future generations struggling with a severe scarcity of resources, their living standards becoming so much lower than ours. Will the people forming these generations have a moral ground for complaint against us? No, because they would'nt have existed at all, as those particular persons they are, had we adopted another and better policy.

This argument has become quite famous in the literature concerning future generations. But I have never been able to see its point. Imagine yourself to be a member of that victimized generation. What would your personal identity have to do with your moral standing as a complainant? You would'nt complain in your capacity of being Peter or Paul, you would complain in your capacity of being a member (among many others) of a group of people placed in a situation which their forebears could have made so much better. The last passage I cited from Feinberg agrees with this. (One wonders also whether it

---

[70] Ibid. Feinberg also discusses the question whether future generations have an *actual* interest: the interest to come into existence. He rightly denies it.

[71] Parfit 1984, 351 f. Cf.the discussion in Achterberg 1994, 197-201. I must desist from discussing Parfit's own (utilitarian) handling of the problem.

really makes sense to ask people to consider the possibility "that they would'nt have existed at all". But I have no room to discuss that rather metaphysical point.)

This situational character of possible grounds for complaint does'nt affect in the least the conceptual necessity (see 3.2.1 and 4.3.2) of considering justice to future generations as a justice meted out to individuals, in the sense of individual places described in terms of an average availability of environmental resources for the people living at a certain point in time.

Let us realize that the non-identity argument sets a frightful moral trap for future generations[72]. Would they ever have grounds for complaint? Its acceptance would also have most curious consequences in other spheres than the environmental one. No doubt many Jews living as our contemporaries would not have been born as the particular inviduals they are, had Hitler not appeared on the scene of history. It is easy to imagine chains of causation linking the one circumstance with the other. Does that mean that they must keep silent on the Holocaust, or even be thankful for its having caused them to be born?

---

[72] In the same sense: Achterberg 1994, 200 and Hilhorst 1987, 75-77. Hilhorst refers to D.MacLean, A moral requirement for energy policies, in D.MacLean, P.G.Brown (eds.), Energy and the Future, Totowa N.J. 1983, pp.180-197.

CHAPTER 4

JUSTICE: A DETACHED PERSPECTIVE

I now discuss the concept of justice between generations that forms the normative core of the sustainable economy. I do so by discussing Rawls on justice between generations.

4.1 WHY JUSTICE?

I claimed right at the start of the present argument that the international consensus on the duty of justice to future generations, which forms the moral core of the sustainable economy, subjects society as a whole to moral judgement. It is on its way to become a fundamentally new starting-point for the definition of social and economic aims.

There is a global distributive intent (sharing the environmental resources of the planet with future generations on a basis of equality) which itself relies on the operation of society as a distributive mechanism. As it is based on a desire of justice, the moral judgment is, in principle, a strict one that tolerates no compromise and puts forward a claim to regulative primacy. Society either shares its resources equitably with its future citizens or it does'nt. Now (as I suggested already in my Introduction), these various elements combine to suggest very strongly the usefulness in our present context of the concept of the just basic structure, which is developed by John Rawls in his theory of justice; for Rawls,

> "the primary subject of justice is the basic structure of society, or more exactly, the way in which the major social institutions distribute fundamental rights and duties and determine the division of advantages from social coope-ration."[73]

Rawls himself gives an intergenerational dimension to this distributive task, by stipulating a principle of just savings.

I now comment in a general way on the postulate of justice between generations. Let me first formulate in a concise form what content I attribute

---

[73] Rawls 1971, 7.

to it. There is a feeling that the resources of the planet, which are finite, must be shared with all generations that will follow us. These resources are considered to sustain life and culture across time, no position in time justifying, by itself, a stronger call on them than any other. The postulate reflects a typically temporal reading of justice in the following ways: (i) it involves a natural understanding of intergenerational succession, i.e. of human society as an on-going affair, (ii) it sees harm being caused by the living to potential people in the structurally time-related form of "not leaving them enough".

The following aspects of the postulate merit attention.

a. The concept of justice is the only one which is capable of giving a plausible form to our intuitions. The utilitarian notion of maximizing happiness is a counter-intuitive one (cf.2.1 above). I share Rawls' general objections against the utilitarian point of view; we must respect the separateness of persons. Let us not forget, in that connection, that the utilitarian calculus of happiness has proved capable, historically, of entering into an unhappy alliance with the totalitarian aspects of social Utopia, which the intuition of intergenerational justice surely bears no relation with. Finally, one does'nt quite see how aggregative considerations could find the framework they need, as particular generational collectives only exist by virtue of arbitrary stipulations on our part (cf.3.2.1 above). Working as the distributive mode of moral objectivity, justice realizes impartiality in a non-aggregative way: it is for future persons that we want to secure equal chances, on a basis of sustained continuity.

b. In stipulating equality, the norm of justice between generations shows its strongly counterfactual character: it neutralizes the power disequilibrium between the present and the future, and thereby meets a structural problem of relations between generations which one needs to deal with in a general way. The impersonal character of the norm is essential to it.

It is remarkable, when one comes to think of it, how differently relations between generations are structured from relations between societies within a common time-frame. On the one hand, conflict is a much more in-built eventuality (future people structurally depend on the living leaving them a livable environment, while societies may co-exist in the world without having anything (or anything much) to quarrel about — take Mongolia and Panama); on the other, the visibility of conflict is much more a function of the moral point of view (justice) itself, as one has to do with people who do not yet exist.

c. No merely humanitarian motives can take the place of justice, the most public and the most legal of the virtues (Hart). I remarked that justice tolerates no compromise and puts forward a claim to regulative primacy; its vocation is to define the basic structure of society. The morally stringent character of justice also comes out in its easy translation in terms of individual or collective rights. It inspires definite claims, based upon a shared measuring-rod for the comparison of relevant states of affairs. This is a very different thing from basing consideration for the interest of future people on feelings of sympathy which we might have for them ("duties of benevolence") — feelings whose discretionary character would prevent the attribution of moral rights to future people, all the more since they surely offer no guarantee of reaching them all without distinction[74].

d."Justice constitutes one segment of morality primarily concerned not with individual conduct but with the ways in which classes of individuals are treated. It is this which gives justice its special relevance in the criticism of law and of other public or social institutions."[75]

It is clear that our relations with future generations typically involve the treatment of a class of individuals, although the processional and open-ended character of this class is a strikingly original one.

e. Justice between generations forms a natural alliance with the search for transgenerationally valid criteria of environmental integrity, established by means offering the best chances for consensus and clear definition. It establishes a norm of equality over time that has no meaning unless a stable measuring-rod is used for comparing different environmental states of affairs. Its detached character points towards "very general human goods", "(whose) value does not have to be seen through the particular values of the individual.."[76] — those last words having to be translated here into: the particular values of one's community or historical epoch. Justice forms the normative platform for trying to define an environmental baseline that is culturally neutral.

f. The just basic structure works through all relevant background institutions: it requires a certain social state of affairs, it does'nt impose particular means for reaching it (except constraints it defines itself, such as the basic liberties and the rule of law). Within our present context of discussion,

---

[74] van der Wal 1979, 13-16, 22-23. Cf.also 5.1.3 hereunder.

[75] Hart 1961, 153.

[76] Nagel 1986, 171.

all measures of environmental protection qualify; so does e.g. the "precautionary principle" adopted as principle 15 in the RIO Declaration:

> "In order to protect the environment, the precautionary approach shall be widely applied by States according to their capabilities. Where there are threats of serious or irreversible damage, lack of full scientific certainty shall not be used as a reason for postponing cost-effective measures to prevent environmental degradation."

g. I already commented upon the indeterminate character of the just basic structure (1.1). Taking our cue from Rawls, we can say that justice to future generations proves a worthwhile concept if it defines the range of justice more in accordance with our considered judgments than do other concepts, and if it singles out with greater sharpness the graver wrongs a society should avoid.

JUSTICE BETWEEN GENERATIONS AND NORTH–SOUTH RELATIONS

The way in which we conceptualize our relations with future generations from a moral point of view cannot be divorced from the way in which we seek to develop new moral patterns within the field of contemporary international relations. As concerns the latter issue, let me mention the current debate about distributive justice on a global scale. This debate has been initiated by the extension of Rawls' difference principle to the world, proposed by Charles Beitz (1979) on the ground that membership of a particular society is morally arbitrary. One of the main areas in which it is being continued presently is the prevention of global warming. The climate change negotiations confirm the relevance of a debate on fair allocations (of costs or of permitted emissions)[77].

Now, if it is justice that indeed provides the right focus for the climate negotiations (and if we widen that premise to include all environmental issues in North-South relations), must one imagine that focus to be another one when it is not environmental relations between nations within the contemporary world that are being contemplated, but environmental relations across time between whole world populations? If fairness has been allowed to structure the one area of concern, no reason can be thought of for not extending it to the other. The two areas very much overlap. Were different basic principles

---

[77] A strong argument in favour of justice being the right focus in the climate negotiations is developed by Shue 1992. His conclusion agrees with the cosmopolitan perspective of Charles Beitz: every human being should be allowed an equal maximum level of greenhouse-gas emissions.

allowed to reign, one does'nt see where the line would have to be drawn between the two. As the search for just arrangements between nations here concerns environmental problems, long-term ecological interests are probably involved from the start; that search itself develops within a time-span that is left undefined; therefore, it would be quite unreasonable to consider persons living at some distance in time as having a lesser claim on the environment on account of that temporal factor than persons one expects to exist next day or next year.

One must notice also that a principal motive for seeking justice is the same in both cases: the counterfactual definition of equal starting positions where no equality is to be found in reality. In a recent contribution, Shue argues that rational bargaining would not meet the ends of justice[78]. If background injustices have produced the weak bargaining position of the poor nations, it is doubly unfair to exploit that bargaining weakness. Shue also argues that the interests which poor nations would be expected to sacrifice are of a different order ("survival interests") than those sacrificed by rich nations.

I just argued in favour of justice between generations on the basis of coherence with global justice within a contemporary time-frame. One more often meets aan argument that goes the other way round. Responsibility for the future should not make us forget responsibility for the present: if our forward-looking duties are based on a commitment to justice, does'nt that same commitment require us to work for more balanced relations within the present world? The connection is a direct one: intergenerational justice cannot be had without an international distribution of the required sacrifices that is equitable. It is true that severe conflicts occur between respect for the urgent needs of the present and respect for the environmental interests of future people. But this emphasizes the need for greater justice between nations: it is through higher levels of welfare that one must minimize and in the end suppress the possibility of such conflicts.

So it would seem that a theory of justice over time cannot be developed without calling for its complement: a theory of justice that makes the present world its constituency.

---

[78] Ibid. Identical objections have been formulated by Brian Barry against the "mutual advantage" model he considers to inspire Rawls' circumstances of justice, see 4.3.3 hereunder.

Other interpretations of the moral point of view

I now want to contrast justice with two other interpretations of what we are committed to when taking the moral point of view in respect of future generations.

HARM

Would it suffice to say simply that we must avoid doing harm to future people? I think one can confidently affirm that there is a "natural duty" (Rawls) not to harm or injure our fellow beings. Could we not regard future environmental damage as an instance of such harm or injury? I think an affirmative answer is in order; the idea of having to share the resources of the planet with our descendants clearly implies that we abstain from causing environmental damage. The one missing factor is the notion of equality. What justice aims at is the conservation of an environmental capital base, in order to sustain life and culture across time on some level of equal opportunity. This of course still leaves a lot to be filled in. But it certainly gives to the concept of relevant harm a more definite content than it would otherwise have.

SOLIDARITY

Another possible competitor is the concept of solidarity. I define solidarity for present purposes as one person or group's act of identification with another person or group, within the limits of some conception of shared interests or of a shared destiny. It should be noted immediately that no judgment of value is attached to the concept: gangsters may very well show solidarity to one another.

I am not sure whether the idea of solidarity does require in common usage the mutual recognition of shared interests or of a shared destiny. In any case, no such mutuality is possible in our relations with future generations. Solidarity in respect of such generations can only be a one-sided act of identification on our part, leading to ecological self-discipline, and based upon the knowledge that we all share the same planet.

But is this an adequate description of the reasons why we should take account of the interests of future populations? Let me mention the following difficulties.

I already noted that no value attaches automatically to the concept. It does not reflect high moral standards by itself, as contrasted with a concept like justice (we should all be just: but should we all show solidarity...with whom?).

So talking about "solidarity" with future generations begs the question from a normative point of view: it does not sufficiently articulate the moral point of respecting the interests of future generations, although it does suggest, in some vague manner, that the rationale behind that concern lies in a shared condition of ecological scarcity. The concept of justice is a much better candidate, all the more since it introduces a distributive criterion (equality) which does not clearly inhere in the concept of solidarity.

A related difficulty, that is masked by the concept of solidarity with future generations, is that solidarity reflects an essentially exclusive point of view: we don't identify with everybody, we identify with the members of a particular group.

> "Solidarity requires identification with those with whom one feels it. For that reason there is always a potentially sinister side to it. It is essentially exclusive. Solidarity with a particular group means lack of identification with, and less sympathy for, those who are not members of that group, and often it means active hostility to outsiders ... "[79].

Now the intuition that we should respect the interests of future generations needs to be articulated in a contrary way. It is not difficult to show that a proper concern for future generations tends to resist the parochial approach. This applies especially to environmental issues because of their strongly holistic characteristics (for instance, global warming respects no frontiers). The further we look into the future, the more we consider the fate of mankind as a whole.

It is within the framework of the view from the present, as discussed in the next chapter, and so of the context of justice (and not in place of justice itself) that the concept of solidarity has a useful part to play. One of the main sources of concern with the future probably consists in identifying with the future members of one's community because that community is implicitly felt to be an on-going entity. But again, this may lead to parochial attitudes that do not agree with the planetary scope of environmental problems.

4.2 JUSTICE OVER TIME AND RECIPROCITY

The concept of reciprocity plays a key role within the present discussion. As its analysis is a complex one, I now attempt to give an overview of its

---

[79] Nagel 1991, 178.

treatment within the confines of the present argument, thus anticipating in a certain measure the more detailed analysis pursued in later paragraphs.

(i) A central thesis of my argument (inspired by Brian Barry) is that justice between generations extends beyond the framework of reciprocity, if the latter term is understood in Hume's sense of individuals living within circumstances broadly characterized by a balance of forces allowing mutual advantage. I consequently criticize Rawls' "circumstances of justice" (which are inspired by Hume) by drawing attention to the strong counterfactual potential of justice. Justice may strive for equality where equality is, as yet, totally absent in social reality.

However, the application of this counterfactual potential of justice to intergenerational relations brings us into unfamiliar territory, as the evident vocation of justice (traditionally insisted upon) is to rule social coexistence. Even when one denies the relevance, for relations between generations, of reciprocity understood as a set of empirical conditions for the meaningful discourse about justice, one still has to deal, in Rawls' theory, with a strong defense of reciprocity as a normative *aim* of the just society: "society" thus being equated, in another sense, with a situation of people living together. So the question arises whether justice, in stepping beyond the bounds of coexistence, is not in some way carried forward by an alternative paradigm of human society. Should one not presume that there is a a wider context of values and interests that orientate it towards the future and which takes the place of the social fullness of life which surrounds justice between contemporaries?.

(ii) I shall claim (also in line with Brian Barry) that Rawls is inconsistent in that he accepts the limitations imposed by Hume on the meaningful use of the concept of justice while fully counting himself, at the same time, on its counterfactual potential (as is manifested by the "original position" and its very egalitarian tendencies, and by its extension to relations between generations as well).

STRUCTURES OF JUSTICE ACROSS TIME

(iii) Now I think it is interesting to notice at this stage that our intuitions of what justice is about directly offer frameworks or structures of justice across time that carry us (at least potentially) beyond relations between contemporaries.

My first example I call the camping ground analogy[80]: it is an intuitively convincing idea that hikers arriving at a campsite must be able to find it clean and with firewood cut and neatly stacked, and that they must leave it in the same conditions. The whole practice of hiking would be undermined if such rules were not observed. This camping ground intuition finds a more general form in the idea of responsible stewardship, which inspires legal régimes like trust or usufruct. One is supposed to maintain a resource at such a level that it remains capable of future use by others. This might be compared in some respects (while accentuating temporal succession) to Locke's principle that when men acquire property by their labour, they must leave enough for others[81]. God has given the earth to humanity as a whole. Man is a creation of God, and must follow God's purpose; so Man cannot dispose of his own life, and everyone should do what is in his power to conserve the life of his fellow man. When we acquire property by the transformation of nature in order to sustain ourselves, we must respect the other man's right to do likewise. One might say that the common denominator here is justice as conservation; the central idea, I think, is that of different interests in a resource, which are spread over time and all have a claim on satisfaction. As nothing in the concept requires that the said interests be had by people who are con-temporaries, it in effect replaces coexistence (and thereby, reciprocity) by succession-in-respect-of-a-certain-resource as the basic fact of life which justice rules with an eye on the fair treatment of all relevant interests.

If we now consider the relations between generations from that particular angle, we can describe them in terms of a formal scheme which some writers term "virtual reciprocity" and which establishes a structure of passing on benefits from one generation to the other. Its general form is as follows. Let us imagine the successive generations A, B, and C. Now what the scheme tells us is that generation B has certain rights in generation A (let us say: rights in a basic respect of its environmental interests), these rights being matched by corresponding obligations towards generation C[82]. Generation B "pays"

---

[80] Achterberg 1994, 190, citing V.D.Lippit and K.Hamada, Efficiency and equity in intergenerational distribution, in Pirages (ed.), The sustainable society, New York 1977.

[81] Locke, Second Treatise, V, 27.

[82] Laslett 1992, 26f suggests the name of "intergenerational tricontract", and remarks on its structural difference with a "two-generational procreational contract" (the plausibility of which he denies) and with the "trust between age-groups" which

generation A by passing on comparable benefits to generation C. It does'nt do so just because it has received those benefits from generation A. Brian Barry observes that it is impossible

"to sustain a completely general principle to the effect that the receipt of a benefit creates a *prima facie* obligation to pass on a similar benefit to others ... If someone offers me a toffee apple, out of the blue, and I accept it, does my enjoyment of the toffee apple create even the tiniest...obligation to distribute toffee apples to others?"[83].

There must have been something more: the intention to start an intergenerational practice that is to the good of all subsequent generations, since it establishes a pattern of passing on benefits in the absence of which no generation would be able to *expect* those benefits from its predecessor generation[84]. So generation B does'nt "just" receive benefits from generation A: it receives them in its capacity of first beneficiary of a practice that has been started by generation A and which it (generation B) considers as a right practice on account of its intended utility for all (except generation A) — the consequent obligation of generation B being to pass on the benefits received to generation C. Generation A could be said to have saved for generation B under the condition that generation B would do the same for generation C, that condition being justified itself by the overarching scheme, and thus having to be imposed again by generation B on generation C, etc. But no judgment is passed, as yet, on generation A's decision either to start the practice or not (a practice from which it derives no advantage itself: it has to stay content with the spiritual benefit of enjoying its own altruistic intentions).

Now let us return to justice as conservation i.e. to the sort of intuition of justice across time that is illustrated by the camping ground analogy. When we use the A-B-C scheme to describe the camping ground relation, we find that we are getting a richer normative content for that scheme than it has on its own. The scheme, considered by itself, formulates a general principle of fairness over time: we should not gain from a practice that has been started on the presumption of its being to the advantage of all (except the first generation), without doing our fair share in continuing it.[85] What the camping

---

underpins the arrangements of the welfare state. He thinks there is much confusion in the matter: ibid. 27.

[83] Barry 1979, 70.

[84] Cf.Rawls 1971, 291 on the just savings principle.

[85] Ibid., 111-112 on the principle of fairness.

ground analogy adds to it is the substantive moral duty of "leaving enough for the next in line", which grounds an obligation to *start* a practice of respectful transmission of scarce resources (if it has'nt been started already), and to maintain it over time.

Does the A-B-C scheme indeed represent a sort of extension of justice as reciprocity (I shall return to that notion in 4.3.3), albeit a "virtual" one? Brian Barry thinks so: if we could establish the actual existence of a practice of looking after the interests of later generations, there would seem to be some sort of case, based on the idea of requital, for holding ourselves obligated to continue it[86]. I think it suffices to postulate here a natural extension of the principle of fairness to relations across time. "Requital" belongs to the conceptual family of reciprocity, but the difference between our context and a context of reciprocity (the latter term being interpreted according to its normal use, as a quality or measure of interactive relations within society) should not be underestimated. Characteristically, the only conceivable sanction against a breach of its obligation to generation C by generation B lies in a posthumous loss of reputation. Everything hinges on each new generation's sense of loyalty.

It is difficult to dissociate the idea of reciprocity from social coexistence and its interactive patterns. When Fuller says that society is not composed of a network of explicit bargains, but that it is held together by a pervasive bond of reciprocity, he manifestly has in mind relations between contemporaries (concepts such as interaction or reversibility of roles would not be capable of functioning otherwise)[87]. So what is interesting about the frameworks we are talking about is that they suggest the need for a wider understanding of the field in which the idea of justice operates.

I think I made it clear that the camping ground analogy finds a direct application to relations between generations. What is still on our agenda is whether it would be appropriate in the present historical circumstances to see it as an instance of the A-B-C scheme. Brian Barry quite rightly observes that no evidence exists of our ancestors having had the intention to start an intergenerational practice of passing on an undamaged ecological capital (on the contrary: his impression is that the only reason why our ancestors did not do more damage is that they lacked the technology to do so). He thinks that what

---

[86] Barry 1979, 71.

[87] Cf.Fuller 1969, 19f. on morality and reciprocity. A sociologist would perhaps stress the basic importance of the anthropological category of exchange.

he calls the "extended" form of justice as reciprocity works at the most as an additional moral input when we have reason for adopting a responsible attitude towards our successors anyway; we may then "be in on the foundation of a practice that will make it more likely that our successors will do likewise"[88]. Now it is clear that the present generation does have a reason for adopting a reasonable attitude: it lies, as was suggested already, in our contemporary ecological predicament. According to Peter Laslett, the "generational tricontract" (A-B-C), as he terms it, "gives formal expression to the conviction that each generational entity must deliver the world to its successors in the condition in which it was received"[89]. It is now that circumstances require us to initiate such an intergenerational practice.

4.3 RAWLS ON FUTURE GENERATIONS: AN OVERVIEW

First principle
Each person is to have an equal right to the most extensive total system of equal basic liberties compatible with a similar system of liberty for all

Second principle
Social and economic inequalities are to be arranged so that they are both:
   (a) to the greatest benefit of the least advantages, consistent with the just savings principle, and
   (b) attached to offices and positions open to all under conditions of fair equality and opportunity.

First priority rule (The priority of liberty)
The principles of justice are to be ranked in lexical order and therefore liberty can be restricted only for the sake of liberty.
... ...

Second priority rule (The priority of justice over efficiency and welfare)
The second principle of justice is lexically prior to the principle of efficiency and to that of maximizing the sum of advantages...
... ...,,[90]

---

[88] Barry 1979, 71-72.

[89] Laslett 1992, 29

[90] I reproduce the final statement of the two principles of justice for institutions (Rawls 1971, 302-303) while leaving out specifications of the priority rules that do not seem relevant for our purposes.

I already cited Rawls on the just basic structure. We now need to have a closer look at his treatment of justice to future generations. In contrast with other important aspects of his theory, the argument on future generations presented in "A theory of justice" has remained largely untouched by his later publications[91]. As it is rather complex, and sometimes obscure, its analysis easily merges into an attempt at critical reconstruction. That is a risk to be taken; the results must speak for themselves.

It is true that in discussing justice between generations, Rawls does not refer (except incidentally) to the environment. The picture of intergenerational relations suggested by his theory is a more peaceful and more traditional one than the image drawn presently by the warnings of ecologists. It is still built on the model of long-term values being served by the repeated transmission of economic and cultural capital from one generation to the other. The reason why justice between generations comes up as an important issue in his theory is that this theory conceives society as realizing justice over time. This makes it necessary to discuss savings, and in particular savings subjected to a test of intergenerational equity.

Now what elements of Rawls' theory of justice can help us (in spite of the change in context) to clarify the intuition of an environmental justice across time? I draw up a short list of the relevant points, while indicating the issues where my argument takes an independent direction.

(i) I already mentioned Rawls' concept of the just basic structure (see 1.1). As intergenerational justice renders judgment on society as a whole, submitting it to a "pre-emptive constraint" (Norton), it must find a place within that structure.

(ii) Justice between generations is a problem with Rawls because he lets the realization of the just society and its continuity depend on intergenerational savings. So *just* savings become an issue. Now the affirmation of a norm of justice between generations, which is shared by people from all over the world with different social and political views, should not be made to depend (as concerns its explication) on a commitment to Rawls' theory of justice as a whole. So I don't take over Rawls' general doctrine on savings; we don't need to link the imperative of environmental conservation, dictated by intergenerational justice, to Rawls' views on the

---

[91] The main account of justice between generations is in Rawls 1971, sections 44 and 45. Rawls' warning in 1993, 20 note 22, that the account in 1971 section 44 is defective, concerns one particular aspect only, cf.1993, 274.

general relation between the realization of a just society across time and material or cultural progress. The fewer assumptions we make, the better. What I consider to be directly relevant to our purposes is the way Rawls defines a moral point of view on relations between generations, such as it forms the framework for his notion of just savings (through the rejection of time preference and the resulting construction of the original position).

(iii) According to Rawls, justice rules the distribution of all-purpose primary goods ("things that any rational man is presumed to want"). It is evident that environmental goods occupy a prominent position within that category (I assume that Rawls would'nt deny it) and that they even form the central issue as far as relations between generations are concerned. My suggestion would be to commit ourselves in our explication of justice between generations to the values of liberty, and to acknowledge the importance of environmental conservation by linking it not to Rawls' doctrine on savings, but to his doctrine of equal liberty (first principle of justice). The fair value of liberty depends on certain material conditions; Rawls allows this, while not giving it a central place in his own argument; now, if we consider the fair value of liberty *across time,* we can say that securing that value is an aim of justice such as it is sought for on the environmental front.

(iv) Rawls conceives justice between generations as justice between individuals differentiated according to their position in time. I take over that notion.

(v) Rawls defends a doctrine of "circumstances of justice" (inspired by Hume) that does'nt square with his forward-looking concept of justice (or so I shall claim). It is by means of a critical discussion of that doctrine that one can best affirm the counterfactual impact of justice between generations, while still considering it as a real challenge to theory that justice then operates beyond the bounds of social co-existence. I deal with the last-mentioned point in chapter 5, on the basis of Rawls' own "present time of entry" condition, and of his normative concept of reciprocity (which is quite different from the empirical one which underlies the circumstances of justice).

(vi) Rawls' theory contains valuable elements for describing the context of justice across time which reflect a broader understanding of the good than is allowed for by his central "thin" theory. I just mentioned his normative concept of reciprocity (discussed by him under the heading of moral psychology and the acquisition of the sentiment of justice); another instance (more supportive of justice between generations!) is the concept of social union, where Rawls explains how the theory of justice connects up with the social values and the good of community[92]. That concept is extended by him to relations across time.

However, certain positions I shall defend in chapter 5 on justice in context may not agree with the spirit of Rawls' central message, as they demonstrate perfectionist leanings. This is particularly the case with the notion that justice between generations in the sphere of the environment, while caring for primary physical conditions of life and culture, by the same token secures a horizon for self-transcending values and so is a condition of life having a meaning.

I now discuss the main parts of Rawls' own theory on justice between generations (4.3.1), criticism being centred on the internal coherence of that theory. The more independent approach, as outlined in the above overview, is developed in the next sections (4.3.2 and 4.3.3).

4.3.1 Rawls' own framework

Let me first ask why the topic of justice between generations makes an appearance at all within the framework of Rawls' theory. Taking our cue from Rawls 1993, we can say that this theory develops a conception of justice based upon a political understanding of the person: as a citizen, the person is interested in being able to identify, and respect, a basic distributive structure of society that operates as a common focus for people following different life philosophies ("comprehensive doctrines"). That political understanding finds its expression in a thought experiment, the "original position", from which the principles of justice (which articulate the basic structure) follow in a direct way. They do so because the original position already embodies (in particular through the "veil of ignorance", which sets morally contingent factors aside) the idea that society should be regarded as a fair scheme of cooperation between citizens conceived as free and equal. The first principle of justice secures freedom by a general stipulation concerning basic liberties; the second submits social and economic inequalities to the now famous "difference principle" (these inequalities are to be arranged "so that they are...to the greatest benefit of the least advantaged") and, in respect of offices and positions, to conditions of fair equality of opportunity.

---

[92] Cf. Mulhall & Swift 1996 for a detailed discussion of the communitarian aspects in Rawls' theory of justice.

At first sight, this conceptual framework does not call for any direct treatment of justice between generations. Most comments on Rawls' theory manage to ignore the latter subject, although Rawls himself devotes two sub-chapters to it in "Theory". So how does the issue come up? The answer lies in an awareness of the *time aspect* that adheres to the realization of the principles of justice:

> "(the) appropriate expectation in applying the difference principle is that of the long-term prospects of the least favored extending over future genera-tions"[93].

These prospects are orientated towards an end stage whose discussion I must leave to economists (i.e. the correct "social minimum")[94]. The essential point for our purposes is that the present generation has to save for its successors if it wants to obey the natural duty to uphold and to further just institutions that is accepted in the original position[95].

> "Saving is achieved by accepting as a political judgment those policies desig-ned to improve the standard of life of later generations of the least advanta-ged, thereby abstaining from the immediate gains which are available"[96].

I shall pay some attention to Rawls' concept of savings and to its relation with environmental matters later on; but it should be clear already that Rawls introduces the issue of justice between generations as an issue of just savings. No precise limits can be defined on what the intergenerational rate of savings should be, but it is possible at least to formulate a moral constraint: the burden of savings should be shared equitably between the successive generations.

So Rawls applies the moral point of view in its distributive form to a dimension he wants us to add to the central core of his argument: justice does not only require freedom and equality between contemporaries (in the manner stipulated by the two principles of justice), an ethos of equality also regulates the realization over time of the just society[97].

> "The life of a people is conceived as a scheme of cooperation spread out in historical time. It is to be governed by the same conception of justice that

---

[93] Rawls 1971, 285.
[94] Ibid. 285-286.
[95] Ibid. 289.
[96] Ibid. 292-293.
[97] Ibid. 289.

regulates the cooperation of contemporaries. No generation has stronger claims than any other."

The work that justice has to do here, its work within the dimension of time, is generated by an issue (the need to save in order to reach the correct social minimum) that is functionally related to the above-mentioned core of the theory, though it claims no significant part in the political understanding of the person that lies at the heart of the latter (so it is ignored by most discussions of Rawls' fundamental intentions). But the conceptual apparatus which Rawls applies to that issue (the original position and its veil of ignorance) is the same. Moreover, as concerns our own subject, it is possible to read in Rawls' argument the implication that it is a *conditio sine qua non* of maintaining an equal liberty over time that there should be a baseline availability of environmental resources.

JUST SAVINGS

The crucial fact, as Rawls sees it, is that realizing justice takes time. It is a long-term affair. Now, this naturally calls for some form of intergenerational cooperation: no long-term prospects of the least favored extending over future generations could of course exist if the living were free to spoil or destroy the economic and cultural resources they have inherited from past generations. Rawls draws the picture of a society progressively raising the standard of civilization and culture by an accumulation of real capital (it must be noted here that "capital" is not only "factories and machines", but also "the knowledge and culture, as well as the technique and skills, that make possible just institutions and the fair value of liberty")[98]. Rawls emphasizes that he does not contemplate an endless process of accumulation: once just institutions have been realized, no further saving is required, except for preserving their material base[99].

---

[98] Ibid. 286, 288. This broad conception of savings also appears in the following formula: "Each generation must not only preserve the gains of culture and civilization, and maintain intact those just institutions that have been established, but it must also put aside in each period of time a suitable amount of real capital accumulation" (ibid., 285).

[99] Ibid. 287, 290. See 285-286 for Rawls' explanation of the "correct social minimum", where no further increase is called for. Rawls also makes the point that "justice does not require that early generations save so that later ones are simply more wealthy"(290). He considers that a high material standard of life may be a "positive hindrance" beyond some point (ibid.). In Rawls 1993, 7, note 5, he again points out that the difference

It is here that the issue of justice arises. How indeed is the burden of saving to be shared between generations? However, Rawls does not think it possible to define precise limits on what the *rate* of savings should be.

> "How the burden of capital accumulation and of raising the standard of civilization and culture is to be shared between generations seems to admit of no definite answer ... It does not follow, however, that certain bounds which impose significant ethical constraints cannot be formulated"[100].

What one must aim for is a fair consideration of the issue; that particular solution may be accepted as the right one which has been found in an impartial way.

REJECTING TIME PREFERENCE

Now, I think that an orderly exposition of Rawls' ideas requires that one introduce at this stage of the argument the topic of "time preference" which Rawls himself discusses in section 45, following section 44 on "Justice between generations". This can be justified as follows. The stipulation according to which the burden of savings must be determined in a fair manner as between generations reflects a prior commitment to the moral point of view. One has opted for impartiality. So let us be clear about the particular impact which the moral point of view has within the dimension of time. It means that the living generation has no right to weigh its own interests more heavily, for the sole reason of their being present (actual) interests, than the interests of future generations. Indeed, no principle of intergenerational savings can be envisaged unless such a time preference is rejected from the start. The living generation is strongly tempted to weigh its own interests more heavily than the interests of future, purely potential people (even when the latter interests do not suffer from uncertainty to any relevant degree). But should every living generation be free to determine its savings for the next generation in such an unprincipled way (for instance, by not taking sufficient account of the circumstance that it has reached a higher level of welfare than earlier generations, thus letting future generations do more work than they should properly do), no common savings process could be made a part of the theory of justice at all.

---

principle does not require continual economic growth: it is compatible with "Mill's idea of a society in a just stationary state".

[100] Ibid., 286

In his book, Rawls imagines an "original position", in which idealized parties, placed in a position of procedural fairness, determine the principles of justice. It is clear that the parties in the original position can have no common basis for deciding about savings so long as they do not take the path of moral impartiality, and thus, of an equitable sharing of burdens over time. The savings process is a cooperative process which cannot start and surely cannot continue unless fair terms of cooperation exist. So Rawls puts the parties in the original position on the right course by a stipulation built into that position itself: they are kept ignorant of their place in history, and consequently of their particular interests.

Rawls first mentions the views of Sidgwick on time preference. Sidgwick argues in respect of an individual's decisions regarding his own life that

> "the mere difference of location in time, of something's being earlier or later, is not in itself a rational ground for having more or less regard for it"[101].

On the strength of the principle of utility, Sidgwick extends this conception of rational choice to the different temporal position of persons and generations. At this point, however, Rawls takes a different path."Since in justice as fairness the principles of justice are not extensions of the principles of choice for one person, the argument against time preference must be of another kind". The relevant argument is, very simply, that time preference is unjust:

> "it means that the living take advantage of their position in time to favor their own interests"[102].

I indicated that Rawls eliminates the option of time preference by means of his description of the original position itself. The parties to that hypothetical contract do not know what period they occupy within the course of history. We will see that Rawls considers those parties (inevitably, I think) to be living persons, who presently "enter" into the hypothetical contract situation and who know that they belong to the living; but this does not make them aware of their actual position in history, no knowledge being allowed to them of the stage of civilization they are in, of their resources etc., and no facts being therefore accessible to them on the basis of which they could determine their particular interests. So there is no reason for them to give any weight to mere position in time. This can also be formulated as follows. Because they take up

---

[101] Ibid., 293.
[102] Ibid., 295.

the standpoint of any period, the parties to the original position cannot consent to a principle that would allow any particular period to discount the importance of states of affairs in a more future period: as they also represent that later period, they would victimize themselves by such a consent[103].

REJECTING THE PRINCIPLE OF UTILITY

Have we now said all that needs to be said in order to get just savings off the ground? Not quite: Rawls makes us aware that the rejection of time preference does not, by itself, lead to justice between generations. It still offers room for the classical principle of utility, as the principle of maximizing total utility also rejects the discounting of future well-being on the basis of pure time preference. But it then adopts an aggregative point of view, according to which the greater advantages of future generations can compensate for present sacrifices. Rawls rejects this point of view.

> "(The) utilitarian doctrine may direct us to demand heavy sacrifices of the poorer generations for the sake of greater advantages for later ones that are far better off"[104].

I think that in explaining our intuitions, Rawls' position on this issue is an easy one to accept. It connects with his person-related view of inter-generational justice.

So when Rawls says that the argument against time preference is "settled" by reference to the original position, that settlement must be clearly understood to follow the anti-utilitarian stance which he thinks the parties to the original position will take[105].

JUST SAVINGS AND ORIGINAL POSITION

Let us now consider just savings more specifically. How is the burden of realizing justice to be shared by successive generations? The problem is that of

---

[103] This seems to me to be a more natural explanation than the rather counter-intuitive "symmetry" suggested in 1972, 294.

[104] Ibid., 287. This calculus of advantages "appears even less justified in the case of generations than among contemporaries".

[105] Ibid., 294.

"agreeing on a path over time which treats all generations justly during the whole course of a society's history"[106].

What one is looking for is a "just savings principle". As I observed already, Rawls lets that principle result from the thought experiment which dominates his whole explanation of the just society: the original position. This is one of the typical cases in which Rawls embodies important normative claims in the way the original position is being defined in the first place. Justice between generations is with us from the start. The rules of this hypothetical contract, which is meant to guarantee a fair determination of the basic structure of society, stipulate that the parties to it are kept ignorant ("veil of ignorance") of personal characteristics or circumstances considered morally contingent i.e. devoid of moral relevance to the decisions they have to take. The veil of ignorance symbolizes an objectivity which we all should try to attain in real life when striving for a just society. Its effect is to set aside those aspects of the social world that seem arbitrary from a point of view. It must

"nullify the accidents of natural endowment and the contingencies of social circumstance as counters in quest for political and economic advantage"[107].

So the burden of realizing justice by the appropriate savings must be determined for each generation in an objective relation to its level of advance. Rawls stipulates that the parties to the original position do not know to which generation they belong in history: so they don't know what is the stage of civilization of their society.

"They have no way of telling whether it is poor or relatively wealthy, largely agricultural or already industrialized, and so on ... .they are to consider their willingness to save at any given phase of civilization with the understanding that the rates they propose are to regulate the whole span of ac‐ cumulation.."[108]. They virtually represent all generations by asking themsel‐ ves what principle "the members of any generation (and so all generations) would adopt as the one their generation is to follow and as the principle they

---

[106] Ibid., 289.

[107] Ibid., 15.

[108] Ibid., 287. See also Rawls 1993, 273: "For when contemporaries are influenced by a general description of the present state of society while agreeing how to treat each other, and the generations that come after them, they have not yet left out of account the results of historical accident and social contingency found within the basic structure".

would want preceding generations to have followed (and later generations to follow), no matter how far back (or forward) in time"[109].

And so the just savings principle can be regarded as an understanding between generations to carry their fair share of the burden of realizing an preserving a just society; there is a scheme of cooperation spread out in historical time.

PRESENT TIME OF ENTRY

We just saw that in the original position the parties do not know their place in history: they do not know what the resources of their generation are, how far it has developed economically or socially etc. So why not go all the way and stipulate that the original position contains representatives from all generations? Rawls rejects that idea; it proves to be an interesting exercise to ask oneself exactly why.

Rawls makes it clear that he prefers the "present time of entry interpretation", which lets the parties know that they are contemporaries[110]. The original position

"is not to be thought of as a general assembly which includes at one moment everyone who will live at some time; or, much less, as an assembly of everyone who could live at some time"; this would "stretch fantasy too far"; "it is important that the original position be interpreted so that one can at any time adopt its perspective"[111].

Now why would that general assembly stretch fantasy too far? I think the last-mentioned formulation tells us why: one must be able to *adopt* its perspective, as a thought experiment one performs i.e. as a moral test one actively applies, in one's capacity of a living person, to the possibly contingent aspects of one's historical situation. And one must consequently be able to return from that high level of objectivity to the daily level of "subjective", historically situated existence. I shall claim at a later stage of this argument

---

[109] Rawls 1993, 274. In note 12, Rawls says that this particular formulation differs from that in Rawls 1971. This relates to certain complexities in the text of 1971 which have no importance for my reconstruction of Rawls' argument. In any case, the said formulation perfectly agrees with the spirit of Rawls 1971, 287-288.

[110] Ibid., 292, referring to 139-140. I take "contemporaries" to mean both a) belonging to the same period, and b) belonging to that same period as living persons — say, as the persons presently reading Rawls.

[111] Ibid., 139.

that what stretches fantasy too far is to imagine ourselves becoming so detached, by means of the thought experiment Rawls calls the original position, that we would'nt know whether we belong to the presently living generation or not. We can go very far in taking a detached view, but we do so while knowing that we belong to the living; the detached view is in in a state of constant tension with the situated one.

Does the need to subject the original position to the present time of entry interpretation (partly) detract from the role we observed it to play in the argument on justice to future generations? At first glance, it does'nt: even if one allows the parties to know that they belong to the living, one still can imagine them to strive for maximum detachment in respect of the position they occupy within history as a process. One considers them to have no knowledge of the relative wealth of their society, and *that* is the key hypothesis in the argument for just savings. Though difficult enough to reach in practice, detachment from one's position in history does'nt seem to require more strenuous efforts from the objectifying impulse than "ignorance" of one's talents, one's position in society, etc. It is one of the principal moves of Rawls' communitarian critics to draw attention to the artificiality of such stipulations. As I said already, I do think myself that the detached point of view is an unstable one. But I think justice between generations can only be explicated if we first allow the detached view to have far-reaching ambitions.

I argued that the present time of entry condition does not, as such, affect the argument for just savings. However, Rawls himself considers it to have the gravest consequences. Let me try to explain this as follows.

> "Since the persons in the original position know that they are contemporaries (taking the present time of entry interpretation), they can favor their genera-tion by refusing to make sacrifices at all for their successors; they simply ack-nowledge the principle that no one has a duty to save for posterity"[112].

But why should that be so? One might argue that it is the simple consequence of the veil of ignorance having to do all the moral work in Rawls' conception of the original position; since the veil of ignorance cannot make the parties unaware of their being contemporaries, in order to force them into a fair regard of the interests of future persons, it seems to leave us with a moral vacuum in that respect. But then the following consideration makes itself felt. Rawls does'nt explain how generational egoism can be a problem which still needs to be cared for at this stage of his argument, since it is

---

[112] Rawls 1971, 140 and 292.

already vetoed by the conceptual framework discussed in the preceding paragraphs.

Indeed, the veil of ignorance does allow the parties to know (as a part of their general fund of knowledge) that society is a cooperative venture across time. The issue of just savings would'nt arise otherwise in the first place; and it is in view of that issue (that is, the issue of defining just savings) that it has been made a feature of the original position that the parties don't know their place in history. They are informed of the general laws and features of society, so they know (through reading Rawls) that realizing the just society, and in particular the difference principle, calls for a long-term social commitment. They understand that this realization is a cooperative venture over time; each generation participates in a common effort directed at a common aim, and it knows furthermore that

> "the savings principle represents an interpretation, arrived at in the original position, of the previously accepted natural duty to uphold and to further just institutions"[113].

Kept ignorant of their particular place in history, the parties then define fair terms of cooperation for the whole length of the savings process. But then, savings being part of what the parties know society to be about, namely to realize justice, and their own position having been defined in such a manner as to secure an agreement on just savings, what conceptual room remains for imagining the parties to be still tempted by generational egoism?

So it it is towards another and different conceptual framework that we must turn in order to understand the risk of generational egoism which Rawls keeps alive in spite of the original position[114]. Brian Barry offers the following explanation. According to him, the present time of entry condition is based on the idea that the principles of justice should be capable of being presented as mutually advantageous in the real world[115]. There can be no mutual advantage between people which the original position would assemble from the past, the present and the future(!). They would not be contemporaries. But then, being contemporaries and knowing that they are, they can decide not to save for

---

[113] Ibid. 289. Cf.5.1.3 hereunder on Rawls and motivation by moral reason.

[114] I also wonder -as an afterthought- whether the hypothesis of generational egoism squares with a certain natural understanding of society as progressively "raising the standard of civilization and culture" (or in any case maintaining its material base) which Rawls seems to assume as the background for the realization of justice over time.

[115] Barry 1989, 195.

posterity. As I argued for already, this makes the primary conceptual perspective which stipulates the realization of justice across time, and which defines the original position, drop out of the picture altogether. It is, as if something should still be done (as if starting from zero) in order to neutralize the parties' dangerous awareness of being on the right side of intergenerational power relations. We will see that Rawls finds a way out by stipulating a "motivational assumption" according to which the parties are presumed to be interested in the welfare of their direct descendants.

THE CIRCUMSTANCES OF JUSTICE

Now what is that other framework which explains Rawls' fear of generational egoism and makes him forget what he has invested in the concept of realizing justice over time? It is the doctrine of "circumstances of justice", which Rawls incorporates into the original position, and which Brian Barry considers to have inspired the present time of entry interpretation in the first place. That doctrine makes the relevance of justice depend on certain social background conditions characterized fundamentally by reciprocity. These conditions are claimed to belong to the general features of social life which the parties in the original position know to exist.

I summarize the doctrine as follows. Rawls presents us a picture of society as a cooperative venture between contemporaries. He stands in the tradition of philosophers like Hobbes and Hume, who have reflected on the anthropological foundations of society. Rawls follows Hume's account when describing the circumstances of justice as the normal conditions under which human cooperation is both possible and necessary, and which the parties to the original position know to exist. Let me suggest the style of that account by mentioning its following elements: individuals coexisting at the same time on a definite territory; individuals roughly similar in physical and mental powers with roughly similar needs and interests, for whom mutually advantageous cooperation is possible; a condition of moderate scarcity; conflicting claims on the resources available, on the basis of needs and interests which yet are complementary in various ways, so that a mutually advantageous cooperation is possible[116].

> "(The) circumstances of justice obtain whenever mutually disinterested persons put forward conflicting claims under conditions of moderate scarcity.

---

[116] Rawls 1971, 126-127.

Unless these circumstances existed there would be no occasion for the virtue of justice..."[117].

THE MOTIVATIONAL ASSUMPTION

We saw that according to Rawls, the present time of entry condition creates a risk of generational egoism. I objected that this conclusion disregards the general framework of intergenerational cooperation and just savings which explains why he is interested in justice between generations in the first place. I then interpreted that conclusion (with Brian Barry) as making a tacit reference to the circumstances of justice: the parties to the original position must be defined as contemporaries ("present time of entry") because a background of interactive relations characterized by reciprocity (Barry says "mutual advantage") conditions the meaningful use of the concept of justice. But if such is the case, the absence of a background of interactive relations between ourselves and future generations must let us conclude that an answer to the risk of generational egoism has still to be found.

Let us follow Rawls' own argument. He first suggests that the problem could be solved by stipulating that the parties in the original position have duties to their immediate descendants. "To say that they do would be one way of handling justice between generations"[118]. But he continues as follows: "However, the aim of justice as fairness is to derive all duties and obligations from other conditions; so this way out should be avoided"[119]. Those "other conditions" are left unexplained[120]. But let us go on: how does Rawls manage to close the door he thinks he has left open to generational egoism?

It is not the condition of mutual disinterest which is a dangerous one (that condition is incorporated from the start in the description of the appropriate initial status quo represented by the original position[121]). The danger lies in the

---

[117] Ibid., 128.

[118] Ibid., 128.

[119] Ibid., 129.

[120] Let me speculate that they refer to chapters 18 and 19 on principles for individuals, and in particular to the requirement that the principles for the just basic structure of society are to be agreed to before the principles for individuals. So justice between generations must be argued for on that first level.

[121] Ibid., 13 and 147-149 for an elaboration of this particular point. Rawls makes clear that the premise of mutual disinterest does not mean that justice as fairness is an "egoistic theory". Once it has helped to define the conditions of rational choice, its work is done: the principles of justice that would be chosen require us in ordinary life

paradigm of social interaction that characterizes the "circumstances of justice". People situated outside that interactive reality are left in the cold.

Rawls finds a way out by drawing relations between generations *within* that circle of reciprocity. He stipulates that the parties enter the original position accompanied by their nearest descendants. There is a "motivational assumption". The parties are assumed to be moved, in their mutual relations as contemporaries, not only by the rational consideration of their own interest, but also by a concern for the welfare of some person in the next generation.

> "The parties are thought of as representing continuing lines of claims, as being so to speak deputies for a kind of everlasting moral agent or institution. They need not take into account its entire life span in perpetuity, but their goodwill stretches over at least two generations. Thus representatives from periods adjacent in time have overlapping interests. For example, we may think of the parties as heads of families, and therefore as having a desire to further the welfare of their nearest descendants. As representatives of families their interests are opposed as the circumstances of justice imply ... ..What is essential is that each person in the original position should care about the well-being of some of those in the next generation, it being presumed that their concern is for different individuals in each case. Moreover for anyone in the next generation, there is someone who cares for him in the present generation. Thus the interests of all are looked after and, given the veil of ignorance, the whole strand is tied together."[122]

Let us be clear about the scope of this assumption. It is not contrary to the parties pursuing their own ends; what Rawls does is to define those ends as including care for one's own descendants. Rawls does not leave the sphere of reciprocity: the only difference is that the parties now bring in, as their own, the interests of their nearest descendants.

So savings seem secured, but as a matter of reciprocal relations between contemporaries! And what about *just* savings?

A PARADOXICAL ARGUMENT

I recall the last phrase of the passage cited above: "Thus the interests of all are looked after and, given the veil of ignorance, the whole strand is tied

---

to consider the rights and claims of others. The combination of mutual disinterest and the veil of ignorance forces each person in the original position to take the good of others into account. Ibid. 129: "(a) conception of justice should not presuppose...extensive ties of natural sentiment".

[122] Ibid., 128-129.

together". I think this phrase is symptomatic of the paradoxical character of Rawls' argument on future generations.

We have on the one hand a "motivational assumption" that forms an addendum to the circumstances of justice. Each generation is supposed to care for the next, within a context of broadly reciprocal relations between contemporaries.

On the other hand, we witness the sudden reappearance ("given the veil of ignorance, the whole strand...") of a direct moral interest in conditions of life of future generations that takes no account of distance in time, and that is therefore independent of the particular sentiments one may have for one's direct descendants. Savings are subjected to an overarching regime based on an equal interest in conditions of life for all generations; justice resists an imprisonment within the limits of the so-called circumstances of justice, even when it is assumed that those circumstances include parental concerns. Intergenerational justice operates beyond the sphere of social interaction, in a milieu (the relations between generations) that knows nothing of equal bargaining power, approximate equality, mutual advantage or the like[123].

Brian Barry objects to the motivational assumption on the ground that it lets justice depend

> "on the actual sentiments of natural concern that people have for their successors. A claim of justice should, rather, be one that can be made by (or in this case on behalf of) certain persons on others as having force even if those on whom the claim is pressed have no sentiments of natural concern for the claimants".

I agree with Barry. What is paradoxical in Rawls' argument is that the general run of his theory, such as it also colours his doctrine of just savings, is based on a different philosophy. We shall see that Rawls considers the moral point of view to offer a reason for action in its own right (5.1.3). In subjecting justice, the distributive form of that point of view, to the background constraints of the "circumstances of justice", he puts himself into the awkward position of having to assume certain natural sentiments in order to put justice on a forward-looking track, while manifestly desiring at the same time to keep true to the fully detached view (veil of ignorance) which has already been applied by his argument to relations between generations.

I shall claim that nothing hinders one, all the same, from recognizing that an interest in the welfare of one's descendants offers a powerful psychological

---

[123] Barry 1989, 180-183.

support for letting oneself be "moved" by the call for justice in respect of future humanity. But this bears no intrinsic relation to the argument for justice.

4.3.2 Finding one's way with Rawls

THE REJECTION OF TIME PREFERENCE

We saw that Rawls rejects time preference. It would be contrary to justice if the living were to take advantage of their position in time. So the original position is drawn up in such a way that they take up the standpoint of each period. Although they are allowed to know that they belong to the living, they are made ignorant of their relative position within the history of society; consequently, they lack the knowledge they would need in order to favour (when deciding on the general rate of savings) the particular period they occupy.

Rawls mentions Sidgwick's argument on time preference. Let us recall that Sidgwick starts with considering the life of the individual. He maintains that rationality implies an impartial concern for all parts of our life.

> "The mere difference of location in time, of something's being earlier or later, is not in itself a rational ground for having more or less regard for it"[124].

This is what Thomas Nagel calls "prudential rationality"- a typical instance of taking the detached view. One chooses a standpoint detached from the present and its perhaps very pressing desires, and decides on the weight to be accorded to all one's interests, present and future. Nagel goes on in a very Kantian vein:

> "(it) is an example of the pursuit of freedom because... we try to stand back from the impulses that press us immediately.."[125].

Rawls himself develops the same theme under the heading of deliberative rationality: we have to see our life as a whole (he defends the concept of a "plan of life"), so that the importance we assign to different parts of our life is not affected by the contingencies of the present[126].

Now, Sidgwick extends this aspect of rational choice to the goods of different individuals situated at different positions in time. But he does so on

---

[124] Rawls 1971, 293.

[125] Nagel 1986, 132. Spinoza already thought so: Ethics IV, prop.66.

[126] Rawls 1971, 416f. What Rawls grounds on deliberative rationality is based by O'Neill 1993 (53) on the narrative identity across time of the individual.

the basis of the aggregative principle of utility. Just as the good of one person is constructed by comparison and integration of the different goods of each moment as they follow one another in time, so the universal good is constructed by the comparison and integration of goods of many individuals. Rawls prefers not to rely on this argument, since in justice as fairness "the principles of justice are not extensions of the principles of rational choice for one person" (see 4.3.1 above on Rawls' rejection of the utilitarian point of view). He settles the issue by means of the conditions of fairness incorporated into the original position. If pure time preference is *irrational* in the case of the individual, it is *unjust* in the case of society[127].

This opposes justice to rationality: a quite understandable opposition within the precise limits of Rawls' discussion, but one which hampers terminology if it is maintained on a more general level. Rawls here equates rationality with Sidgwick's utilitarian views on rational choice. But is'nt justice itself a specific mode of the detachment we find invested in moral reason? Of course, "being rational" as an individual in regard to one's own future has no intrinsic relation to morality. But when it is the goods of different individuals we have to reckon with, that same stance of impartial concern clearly forms the core of the moral point of view (it also forms the starting-point of utilitarian morality).

Justice is the distributive mode of moral reason. Time preference is unjust because it destroys the very basis for equality by rejecting the equal consideration of interests — in other words, by rejecting the moral point of view[128]. It is an instance of pure arbitrariness. Justice can have no hold on relations between generations unless impartiality over time has first been firmly put into place. When making use of the concept of justice, we tacitly consider distance in time to be morally irrelevant, thus admitting future, purely potential people to the moral constituency. Future people are recognized as moral selves with an equal claim on respect.

This is recognized in the literature, where a consensus reigns on condemning the practice of discounting future harms or benefits i.e. downgrading their importance according to their degree of temporal remoteness[129]. Yet, "we cannot escape the limitations of our psychology"

---

[127] Ibid., 294.

[128] Cf.Hart 1961, 156 on the connexion between the concept of justice and the very notion of proceeding by rule.

[129] I found the most extensive argument for rejecting time preference (albeit in an utilitarian framework) in Birnbacher 1988, 28-91. Cf.also Cowan & Parfit 1972 or

(Glover). Although any explanation of our intuitive sense of justice must consider it to have rejected implicitly pure time preference, practical life shows all the same that there is a strong psychological and social tendency to discount the value of future interests, as compared with the weight we attribute to identical concerns whose greater merit only consists in being present or proximate ones[130].

The emotional responses that are natural to us diverge from our moral beliefs. So Jonathan Glover, in his stimulating book on modern moral dilemmas, asks how that tension should be dealt with. Must rationalist philosophy "be replaced by a celebration of the spontaneous and the intuitive"?[131] A well-known instance of divergence between the rational and the emotional is provided by the trapped miners example, which contrasts known and statistical lives. Imagine a mining company whose financial position forces it into a choice between rescuing a few trapped miners now and spending the money on an improved warning system so that many more miners would thereby be saved in the long run[132]. A preference for saving the miners now is very much to be expected in actual life (the contrary choice might even entail legal liability). Time bias is strengthened in such a case by the lack of emotional response to the fate of people about whom nothing is known (a factor of indifference which is itself compounded in the case of future generations!).

But is it possible, perhaps, to rise above the empirical level of our actual responses and to contemplate a *moral* argument justifying a preference for the "here and now"? Let me emphasize that a positive answer, if accepted without the right sort of qualification, would squarely contradict the moral point of view as I understand it here, and which the affirmation of justice is an embodiment of.

So I turn again towards Rawls' firm stand on time preference, and consider some more arguments that speak for it. In his discussion of the trapped miners

---

O'Neill 1993, 49f. I myself have no room to discuss the economic side of the argument on time preference.

[130] Cf.Birnbacher 1988, 173-196 for the psychological limitations that affect the consciousness of future states of affairs and its role as a determinant of human action. See also Glover 1977 for the whole chapter on "moral distance" (286f.), where time bias figures as one of the many psychological obstacles to moral reason.

[131] Glover 1977, 294.

[132] I am indebted to Fried 1970, 207f (The value of life). The same example is also discussed by Glover 1977, 210-213. I suppose the example is very artificial because insurance would in most cases take care of the problem. But who knows?

example, Charles Fried takes issue with the personalist argument, which justifies the preference for known lives by virtue of the fact that it is with known lives that we enter into relations of love and friendship, while to the abstract lives we stand in relations defined by justice and fairness; now, according to that personalist argument, relations of love and friendship justify a greater concern, as it is important for human beings to be able to realize such personal relations in significant ways[133]. I summarize Fried's objections as follows. First (but that is less relevant to our relations with future generations): we will later stand in exactly the same relation to those in future peril as we stand presently to those in present peril. Second: love and friendship do not justify disregarding obligations of justice and fairness, the beneficiaries of which are, after all, real persons too.

"The generosity of love and friendship is based on giving up what is one's own, not in depriving a third person of his just and fair entitlements"[134].

Fried's objections seem to dispose of the issue as a moral issue; what is left is the emotional difficulty of looking away from present hardship. But I wonder whether this is not going a bridge too far. Real life presents too many cases in which the claim of immediacy, as Nagel terms it, is likely to win, that victory being accompanied by a vague (though frequently strong) feeling of moral legitimacy. I said in my Introduction that a dynamic conception of ethics must recognize the reality of certain subjective reasons (in our case: the immediate or proximate character of urgent needs) which enter into competition with the claims of a moral point of view defined exclusively in terms of objectivity. Those reasons are a factor in our moral life none the less. A useful framework is offered here by Thomas Nagel, when he draws attention, in his "View from nowhere", to the reasons which may challenge within the field of ethics "the hegemony of neutral reasons and impersonal values". What is interesting for our purposes is that Nagel's aim is not to ban subjective reasons from the sphere of ethics; on the contrary, he thinks ethics is a complex subject because its central problem is

---

[133] Fried 1970, 222f

[134] Ibid. Glover 1977, 211, discusses an argument for saving the men presently trapped in the coalmine that is based on "reaffirming our belief in the sanctity of human life". His comment is that this "suggests that the best way of "reaffirming our belief in the sanctity of life" is by adopting a policy which saves fewer lives than we could save for the same trouble and expense." Cf.also Birnbacher 1988, 232-233, criticizing Callahan; cruelty does'nt exist only within face-to-face relations.

"how the lives, interests, and welfare of others make claims on us and how these claims...are to be reconciled with the aim of living our own lives"[135].

So there exist several types of respectable reasons which are relative to the moral agent and which compete with an ethical perspective centred exclusively on the detached point of view ("a fully agent-neutral morality is not a plausible human goal")[136]. Nagel mentions inter alia (though in a guarded fashion) the "special claim of immediacy, which makes distress at a distance so different from distress in the same room" (this certainly applies to temporal distance)[137]. Ethics are characterized by an unsolved confrontation between the objective and the subjective standpoints. This leads to the realistic conclusion that full objectivity is an aim of moral progress rather than something we may already consider to reign, on the level of principle, for testing all moral conduct in the present world.

So one would have to accept the reality of a measure of pragmatic inconsistency within the field of our moral responses themselves. Even though an obligation to the future can be established, it is possible to imagine situations where the legitimate claims of present and future conflict, and where a choice must be made between them. Such a conflict is a very real one as concerns the environment in certain developing countries, inasmuch as certain urgent needs can only be satisfied there at the expense of long-term ecological interests. What such situations reveal, in effect, is a tragic limitation of the actual scope for intergenerational equity: there just are'nt enough environmental resources to distribute between the present and the future. The present then naturally comes first: should we expect it to commit suicide? The relevant literature often tries to maintain a certain unity in moral perspective by relating the lesser weight of future interests to their uncertainty. We then have a reason for letting present needs weigh more heavily. I am sure this is an important point, but it cannot explain away the eventuality of sharp conflicts between the needs of the present and those of the future. Those needs of the

---

[135] Nagel 1986, 164.

[136] Ibid., 152f.

[137] Ibid., 176. One should note that the claim of immediacy is often strengthened by its being combined with another category of possibly respectable subjective reasons (see ibid., 165): the special obligations we have toward those to whom we are closely related, toward the community we presently live in etc. Cf.Cowen & Parfit 1972, 149-150: the authors apply such reasons to the intergenerational level but make an exception for the infliction of grave harms.

future may be very basic from a biological point of view, and so claim a firm status in our predictions.

How should social ethics respond within the framework of our subject of inquiry? I think that it should hold fast to the intuitive concept of justice between generations, and explore the ways and means of securing a moral harmony based on the fullest actualization of that concept. Two very different approaches can be imagined here, one on the level of ethics themselves, the other on the level of politics.

(i) The rationalist position (also shared by Fried) is summarized by Glover.

"We cannot see any justification for downgrading people because they live far away or in the future, and yet we cannot escape the limitations of our psychology. Our beliefs start to diverge from the emotional responses natural to us." Now "(it) is hard to tell how far it is in our power to modifiy some of our deepest intuitive responses ... ..Critical discussion can at least enable us to withhold our intellectual assent from some of our emotional attitudes, and this may help to weaken the grip they have on us."[138]

Fried's criticism of the personalist argument, which denies the moral standing accorded by the latter to the claims of immediacy, is an instance of such a critical discussion. It is perhaps possible to suspect, behind sympathy for the immediate and the personal, a general conception of ethics which tends to situate the essence of "moral" conduct within the domain of face-to-face relations. Love, friendship, the exercise of many virtues, all seem to call for a measure of proximity. It is stimulating to oppose, to this way of looking at the substance of morality, the general thesis which the French philosopher Paul Ricoeur develops in an essay on the concept of the "neighbour": Ricoeur defends the point of view that it is wrong to work with a moral scheme opposing, to our fellow man ("notre prochain"), the anonymous, social other person (the "socius", as he terms it)[139]. The unmediated encounter between persons is a fleeting and fragile event: it wants to find a stable and durable form. It would even be right to claim in many instances that we only discover the true aim of moral concern when we see other people as the victims of a shared misfortune (exploitation, racial discrimination etc.). My neighbour then is in the plural, so to speak. Love reaches out to a suffering collection of people ("un corps souffrant"). This theme is given a central role by Ricoeur

---

[138] Glover 1977, 295.

[139] Ricoeur 1955, 213f.

within the dialectical interplay between the "near" and the "far" which characterizes moral life.

(ii) I have suggested that a possible avenue for securing the chances of the
detached view against the prestige of the "here and now" consists in critical
reflection. The way we think about ethics may influence our natural responses.
But when we consider the dilemmas we face in our present world, all this
sounds very theoretical. Giving a more central place to impartiality across time
may involve important sacrifices; it may at the limit be impossible because
there is'nt enough to go round anyway. So the most urgent question is not how
we change thinking about such things, but how we *change the world* in order
to exclude (or at least soften) those dilemmas. What I mean is that justice
between generations necessarily calls for a state of affairs which rules out the
possibility of an insoluble clash of interests between present and future needs
(the sustainable society must be able to achieve a proper balance between the
two!).

The political character of achieving moral harmony is emphasized in a
general way by Thomas Nagel when he says that we must devise a political
situation in which the great bulk of impersonal claims is met by institutions
functioning "as a moral buffer to protect personal life against the ravenous
claims of impersonal good"[140]. The impersonal standpoint is just as essential
to the makeup of each of us as the more personal one; "it must be given
adequate expression through our respective roles in impartial collective
institutions..."[141]. So what this is leading us to is political theory: there can be
no ethics without politics. On the other hand, "moral harmony and not only
civil peace is the right aim of politics"[142].

I now make a short and rather tentative comment on the issue whether
discounting the importance of long-term harms in proportion to their (lack of)
probability can be squared with intergenerational justice. Let us imagine that
we have reasons to believe that if radiation escapes four hundred years hence
from some nuclear waste dump, it will be much less likely to cause deaths (for
instance, we expect that some kind of countermeasure will be invented). I
think there is an intuitive rightness in considering that our concern may

---

[140] Nagel 1986, 174.

[141] Nagel 1991, 53f.

[142] Cf.Nagel 1986, 188, 206-207.

decrease proportionately[143]. But I think the prior question is a more interesting one: whether we are justified in imposing risks on posterity at all. Probabilities help us in deciding what risks we want to take ourselves — but then, debits and credits affect the same person (or group of persons). Do we, the living, have the right to impose risks on future people who have not asked for it ? It might be argued that any form of technology we pass on to posterity is based on the acceptance of certain risk levels (for instance, we might decide that nuclear energy still is the better option, in view of the climate problem). Passing on no risks at all would mean returning to pre-industrial times (and exchanging one sort of risk for another). So what is more to the point is the exercise of prudence in respect of worst possible outcomes: the greater the harm that may conceivably occur, the lesser is the relevance of its (im)probability. Playing it safe is an aspect of justice. It is evident, in particular, that irreversible decisions should be avoided as a matter of principle[144].

Let me recall here the precautionary principle adopted as principle 15 in the RIO Declaration (see 4.1 above): where there are threats of serious or irreversible damage, lack of full scientific certainty shall not be used as a reason for postponing appropriate measures of prevention.

A NOTE ON OBJECTIVITY

I think it is important to note that when impersonal values cause us to look forward into the future, they implicitly reject time bias. Let us consider for instance a long-term research project that will certainly go on beyond our own lifetime. It clearly would be absurd to claim that later developments in that research have a lesser value than earlier ones just because of that greater remoteness in time. These later developments may have lesser value for us personally — we perhaps may not live to see them. But impersonal value takes over. The experience we have in working for the project is not the ex-

---

[143] Cf.Cowen & Parfit 1972, 147. But this should of course be distinguished very clearly from attributing a lesser importance to future deaths (as compared to proximate ones) for the sole reason that they are *future* ones.- O'Neill 1993, 50-51 argues against the relevance of the whole issue of discounting. While uncertainty about specific preferences of future generations does exist, uncertainty about their needs does not. Moreover, he claims that no probability functions at all can be ascribed to the uncertainty of future benefits and costs (one reason of that is that the future progress of science is unpredictable). I leave it to more competent persons to discuss that argument.

[144] Cf.in 2.5 Hans Jonas on "future ethics".

perience of something having value "for us" in particular: it is the experience of a good that transcends our lifetime. What counts is our hope that the project will succeed. In respect of such values (and of the harms that form their negative expression), all moments of time enjoy *prima facie* an equal status; so ranking the relevant states of affairs according to their position in time in relation to ours can only be justified, if at all, by reasons provided by the particular good itself (for instance, a particular phase of the scientific project may be more important than another because of the way the project is set up). Time preference is incompatible with respect for the objectivity of the good and so amounts to disrespect towards the good as such. Consequently, having an interest in future impersonal good works as a general support for the moral point of view. But it remains to be seen in every instance whether the way in which the good structures time is compatible with justice. It surely is not when it assumes totalitarian proportions and imposes intergenerational sacrifice.

ENVIRONMENTAL GOODS, PRIMARY GOODS AND EQUAL LIBERTY

In Rawls' theory, justice rules the distribution of all-purpose "primary goods", "the things that every rational man is presumed to want" ("rights and liberties, opportunities and powers, income and wealth")[145]. It is evident that satisfactory environmental conditions must figure conspicuously within that category: we all depend on the natural resources of the planet for sustaining life and culture. Accordingly, one cannot read Rawls on just savings without assuming the integrity of the environnment to be involved as a matter of course. Future life on this planet according to minimum requirements of human dignity is a function of environmental goods being kept available at certain levels from one generation to another, as all-purpose material (biological, physical) resources. No long-term prospects could exist for the least-favoured if the living were free to spoil or destroy the resources they have inherited from past generations. It would be contrary to a fair distribution of the burden of saving if the living generation were to destroy or diminish the ecological basis of future life. Rawls himself clearly suggests that environmental impacts on the welfare of future generations

---

[145] Rawls 1971, 62, 92.

must be met by measures of conservation as a part of the larger societal commitment to just savings[146].

But this perception of environmental goods as primary goods within Rawls' own theoretical scheme must share the limitations of the latter in respect of the environmental context. I said in my overview of Rawls on future generations that the affirmation of a norm of justice between generations should not be made to depend (as concerns its explication) on a commitment to Rawls' theory of justice as a whole. This applies all the more since Rawls' empirical presuppositions are not the right ones for our purposes. He still argues in the traditional terms of a transmission of capital from one generation to the next, while environmental concern may require us to face directly the fate of people remote in time.

Now we can dissociate the interpretation of environmental goods as primary goods from the doctrine of just savings and connect it to another central element of Rawls' theory: the doctrine of equal liberty. We can do so by reading Rawls on the fair value of liberty, and by realizing that environmental goods play a central role in securing the fair value of liberty across time.

Though the separate treatment of equal liberty (first principle of justice) and of justice in the socio-economic sphere (second principle of justice) does'nt suggest so on first consideration, Rawls is quite aware of the circumstance that freedom has no substance unless it translates into a decent spectrum of life options. There is an issue of the fair value ("worth") of liberty. Liberty is represented by the system of the liberties of equal citizenship, while the worth of liberty is proportional to the capacity of persons to advance their ends.

> "Freedom as equal liberty is the same for all; the question of compensating for a lesser than equal liberty does not arise. But the worth of liberty is not the same for everyone."[147]

Some have greater means to achieve their ends than others. Rawls takes account of this as follows. In his "Theory of justice", he restricts his "special conception of justice", which forbids exchanges between basic liberties and economic or social benefits, to societies in which those freedoms can be en-

---

[146] Ibid., 296: "causing irreversible damages" is described as a "grave offense" against other generations. See also ibid., 137, 271.

[147] Ibid., 204. The "fair value of liberty" is also mentioned at 288, 290 and 298.

joyed[148]. In the first lecture of "Political liberalism", warning the reader that important aspects of the principles of justice are left out in his discussion, he says that in applying the first principle covering the equal rights and liberties one must assume a lexically prior principle requiring that citizens' basic needs be met, at least insofar as their being met is necessary for citizens to understand and to be able fruitfully to exercise those rights and liberties[149].

A baseline availability of environmental goods surely figures among those basic needs. Let us now concentrate on the intergenerational dimension, which Rawls himself draws attention to in this sphere when he observes that by causing irreversible damages, the living generation may perpetuate grave offenses against other generations[150]. Once focused upon by the doctrine of just savings, that dimension makes us also consider the fair value of liberty in the temporal perspective of *maintaining* its value across time. Let me recall here how an argument based on the affirmative duties of the modern state leads to the conclusion that government must secure the physical basis of the liberties of its future citizens by the appropriate measures of environmental protection (2.3).

Liberty has no substance unless it translates into a decent spectrum of life options. Brian Barry formulates it as follows:

> "(what) justice requires...is that the overall range of opportunities open to successor generations should not be narrowed. If some openings are closed off by depletion or other irreversible damage to the environment, others should be created...to make up"[151].

The connection with equal liberty raises the following issue. We saw that Rawls' principles of justice together constitute the just basic structure of society, and so claim a regulative primacy: they tolerate no trade-offs with

---

[148] Ibid., 151-152.

[149] Rawls 1993, 7. In 1971, 204 and in 1993, 326-329, Rawls expresses a confidence in the difference principle which leads to opposite conclusions. A lesser worth of liberty is compensated for, says Rawls, since the capacity of the less fortunate members of society to achieve their aims would be even less were they not to accept the existing inequalities whenever the difference principle is satisfied. So Rawls rejects as superfluous the idea of a fixed bundle of primary goods to be secured to each citizens. I take it that this must be read in conjunction with the assumption of a minimum level of welfare which Rawls makes in respect of the basic liberties in 1971, 151-152.

[150] Rawls 1971, 296.

[151] Barry 1978, 243.

other social aims. Now, Rawls introduces, within that just basic structure, a second, internal priority rule by stipulating that the first principle of justice ranks prior to the second principle, which regulates social and economic inequalities. There is a lexical order between the two, in the sense that the first principle must be satisfied before one moves on to the second: liberty can only be restricted for the sake of liberty. The question is, whether it is necessary to rely, in our own context of inquiry, on that specific lexical priority, once the general regulative primacy of the just basic structure as a whole (and so of justice between generations as a part of that structure) has been firmly recognized. Is there some advantage in letting equal rights on environmental resources (insofar as these resources are essential to the fair value of liberty) share such an "internal" higher status?[152] I think a positive answer is in order, *if* one considers it (with Rawls) to be a necessary part of one's doctrine of justice to join, to the basic liberties, a regulation of social and economic inequalities such as the difference principle is an example of. Now I said, in my overview of Rawls on future generations, that the fewer assumptions we make, the better. The intuition of intergenerational justice is shared on a world basis: so its explication cannot be loaded with a too heavy theoretical baggage. I suggested that we limit ourselves, for the purpose of that explication, to a paradigm of equal liberty (Rawls' first principle of justice). The argument for justice between generations does'nt need to commit the just basic structure to Rawls' second principle.

JUSTICE FOR INDIVIDUALS

I observed that according to the processional model proposed by Laslett and Fishkin for throwing some light on the diffuse concept of "generations", justice over time would have to be construed as justice between individuals, the titles "generations", "age groups" and "cohorts" serving only as indefinite indicators of persons in similar temporal positions (3.2.1). This structural argument is reinforced by a moral one when Rawls rejects the principle of utility (4.3.1). Should we accept the latter principle, it would still be possible to contend that particular generations must sacrifice their interests to an intergenerational maximization of happiness or to the realization of some grand historical scheme. But according to Rawls, the end stage of just savings

---

[152] In that sense: Singer 1988.

"is not to be thought of as that alone which gives meaning and purpose to the whole process. To the contrary, all generations have their appropriate aims. They are not subordinate to one another any more than individuals are. The life of a people is conceived as a scheme of cooperation spread out in historical time. It is to be governed by the same conception of justice that regulates the cooperation of contemporaries. No generation has stronger claims than any other."[153]

So the principle that results in our case is a principle of equality in respect of basic environmental resources between individuals differentiated according to their position in time. What one asserts is that the individuals situated in the year 2200 may not be discriminated against, in respect of a moral claim on such resources, in favour of the individuals situated in the year 2100 or in the year 2000. No concepts exist which would make it possible to define, in a non-arbitrary manner, separate generations as separate collective bodies entitled to equal shares in the resources of the planet. What one is dealing with is individual "places", although individualization here probably presents its own problems. One is tempted at first to conceive, straightaway, *average* life chances determined according to the resources available at a certain moment for a certain number of people (the population factor thus appearing to be a vital one). But I must leave it to further discussion whether that notion of average life chances agrees with the non-distributive character of important environmental goods and with the possible absence in certain cases of a direct relation with population numbers.

Let me remark, for the sake of clarity, that the absence of general concepts for identifying generational collectives forms no obstacle to a differentiation between people according to their position in time that follows from the intrinsic nature of some particular ecological issue. For instance, one can imagine a forecast concerning the development of some environmental hazard, which identifies people situated within an approximate future period as being specially affected.

4.3.3 Criticizing Rawls' "circumstances of justice"

I observed that there is certain lack of coherence in Rawls' theoretical model, because the background conditions of justice as Rawls describes them ("unless these circumstances existed there would be no occasion for the virtue of justice") cannot obtain on the general and ambitious level of

---

[153] Ibid., 289. Cf.also ibid., 505: it is to persons that the guarantees of justice are owed.

intergenerational objectivity which finds its expression in the original position. The demonstration is easy. Let us admit as a general proposition that a conflict of interests is the necessary occasion for an intervention of distributive justice. Now a competition for scarce resources does not *exist* between generations unless the presently living generation is willing to grant a claim to future people in the first place. As this willingness derives from its sense of justice, it follows that justice precedes (so to speak) the "circumstances" that are said to be antecedent to it!

What clearly emerges is that one must gain a clear view of the counterfactual nature of justice, by rejecting the philosophy that is at the bottom of the circumstances of justice. I gladly refer to Brian Barry's criticism of the latter concept, which according to him centres on the idea of persons seeking mutual advantages from more or less comparable bargaining positions[154]. Based on Hume's account of justice, the doctrine reflects a contractualist view on social relations. Justice is a matter of conventions we enter into when power differentials are not so important as to make such agreements an irrational choice; it is understood as the solution to a problem that is now currently expressed in the language of games theory. To this conception of justice as mutual advantage, Barry prefers the idea of justice as impartiality. As he formulates it,

> "the desire to be able to justify our conduct in an impartial way is an original principle in human nature", which directly applies to our relations with future people[155].

That original principle has no need for antecedent circumstances such as those which are stipulated by Rawls in line with Hume. According to Brian Barry, when Rawls puts justice between generations on his agenda, he steps from "justice as mutual advantage" to "justice as impartiality" and thus makes his theory suffer from a strong inner tension[156].

---

[154] Barry 1989, 179-183, 189-203.

[155] Ibid., 364.

[156] Barry 1978 and 1989. Cf.also Rawls 1993, 17: Rawls counters Barry's interpretation of "reciprocity" in terms of "mutual advantage" by showing, as concerns the difference principle, that an equalizing form of justice is being made to work first of all (see also Rawls 1972, 103); "the aim is to specify an idea or reciprocity between free and equal citizens in a well-ordered society". So what we get in the end (and this of course loads the dice still more against the "circumstances of justice") is a purely normative concept of reciprocity, which leaves full room for the counterfactual potential of justice : see 5.1.2 hereunder.

If we follow the lead of our intuitions concerning future generations, we must indeed be able to conceive of justice as correcting situations of asymmetry by a grant of equal rights within social contexts which show an imbalance in power and resources that may at the limit result in total domination. It is such a redress that is needed in the relation between the presently living generation and future ones, particularly in the ecological sphere, in order to ensure equal opportunities for future people. No antecedent conflict of interests between more or less equivalent forces can exist here, because the living are all-powerful[157].

The picture suggested by the circumstances of justice is one of conflicting claims put forward on a basis of approximate social symmetry; accordingly, should an individual or group of individuals have no other resource than to appeal to the moral feelings of a dominant party, this could not be described otherwise than as an appeal to charity. The *locus classicus* for such a view is to be found (in its more elegant form) in Hume's "Enquiry concerning the principles of morals". I cite the relevant passage in its entirety.

"Were there a species of creatures, intermingled with men, which, though rational, were possest of such inferior strength, both of body and mind, that they were incapable of all resistance, and could never, upon the highest pro-vocation, make us feel the effects of their resentment; the necessary conse-quence, I think, is that we should be bound, by the laws of humanity, to give gentle usage to those creatures, but should not, properly speaking, lie under any restraint of justice with regard to them, nor could they possess any right of property, exclusive of such arbitrary lords. Our intercourse with them could not be called society, which supposes a degree of equality; but absolute command on the one side, and servile obedience on the other. Whatever we covet, they must instantly resign: Our permission is the only tenure by which they hold their possessions: Our compassion and kindness the only check, by which they curb our lawless will: And as no inconvenience ever results from the exercise of a power, so firmly established in nature, the restraints of jus-tice and property, being totally *useless*, would never have place in so unequal a confederacy."[158]

Again, the notion of justice in respect of future generations cannot be consistently entertained unless one proves such an account to be wrong. Brian Barry shows that it clashes with our clearest intuitions. Writing before the end of apartheid, he lets us see what it amounts to by asking us to imagine

---

[157] Barry 1978, 223: "(there) can be no getting round the total absence of equality".

[158] Hume 1767, 256-257.

"someone who, asked whether or not South African policies are unjust, re-
plied that the answer would depend on an estimate of the white's ability to
hold down the rest of the population indefinitely."[159]

Clearly, it is a counterfactual move that is expected here and elsewhere;
how could one otherwise explain the rights of infants or handicapped persons?

Brian Barry has argued in an earlier article that the framework within
which we normally think about justice — the framework that serves us well
enough for thinking about relations among contemporaries in the same society
— fails to give us a grip on problems of intergenerational justice[160]. That
framework is: justice as reciprocity. Every society has some notion as to the
rightness of meeting reasonable expectations that a favour will be returned, of
pulling one's weight in cooperative enterprises, of keeping agreements that
provide for mutual benefits, and so on. Barry develops his analysis of justice
as reciprocity under three headings: justice as requital (making a fair return for
benefits received), justice as fidelity (carrying out one's side of a bargain
voluntarily entered into), and justice as mutual aid (playing one's part in a
practice of helping those in need).

It is clear that we run into immediate difficulties when we try to apply this
paradigm of justice to relations with future generations, just as we do when we
try to apply it to problems of justice between nations.

"The glaring limitation of justice as reciprocity is that it can say nothing about
the initial control over natural resources. Once ownership rights are assig-
ned..(it)..can tell us about fair trading. But it is silent on the crucial first stage."[161]

So one is supposed to be capable of saying what is fair trading between
Somalia and the US without bringing in any question of initial advantage!
As concerns relations across time, what we get is a blank cheque for any
given generation to use the earth's resources as it sees fit.

Barry finds a solution by drawing attention to another conception of
justice, complementary to justice as reciprocity, and also deeply rooted in our
common ideas: equality of opportunity (which translates, in our context, in
equal access to the earth's natural resources)[162]. Let us recall here the camping
ground analogy (4.2 above)!

---

[159] Barry 1978, 222.
[160] Barry 1979, 51.
[161] Ibid., 73.
[162] Ibid., 51, 75f. A remark on terminology: I take it that "mutual advantage" in Barry
1989 can be equated with "justice as reciprocity" in Barry 1979, and that "justice as

Symmetry not as a condition, but as an aim of justice: this idea can be rooted in an understanding of the golden rule that makes it express a *norm of mutual recognition* applied to circumstances characterized by social a-symmetry[163]. Such an understanding lets the essential point of morality consist in the prohibition of violence; what morality does (in Kantian terms) is to prohibit an imposition of the will that violates the other man's dignity conceived as an end in itself. It is that primal prohibition that inspires (more or less directly) the critical attitude in respect of social inequality.

So the lack of symmetry does not come in the way of an appeal to justice, it forms its prime occasion. It is the artificiality of the virtue of justice, its counterfactual impact, which forms its most precious contribution to social life[164]. This theme has been well explored by Goodin, who derives obligations to future generations from the very difference in power between the generations. The vulnerability of future generations, their complete dependence on the living, provides the reason for our obligations to them[165]. I think this agrees with familiar feelings. That the elimination of the worst sufferings and deprivations comes first according to common moral sense surely derives in a great measure from the importance we feel it to have for personal autonomy and dignity.

It is an interesting question whether the contrast between such an account of justice and Hume's paradigm of "utility" (.."as no inconvenience ever results from the exercise of a power, so firmly established in nature..") reflects some fundamental divide in the history of the concept. The French philosopher Henri Bergson has hinted as much: according to him, the history of moral sense can be characterized as the evolution from a "closed" morality ("morale close") to an "open" one ("morale ouverte"), which lets a form of justice that applies to exchanges (or, more generally, to relations of reciprocity) be transformed into a more generous conception that is quite

---

impartiality" in Barry 1989 covers the same ground as "equality of opportunity" in Barry 1979.

[163] Ricoeur 1990, 255-256. Ricoeur interprets the golden rule from the perspective of the second Kantian imperative. A very similar idea is developed by Rawls when he says that by acting on the principles of justice, "men express their nature as free and equal rational beings".

[164] Comte-Sponville 1995, 107f.

[165] Goodin 1985, 277.

independent of such background conditions because it consists in affirming the inviolable rights of the person[166].

There is no difficulty in combining agreement with the above criticism of the circumstances of justice with the idea that there is a formal sense — quite independent of social symmetry -in which it is true that we have no occasion to exercise the virtue of justice unless we face a situation of persons putting forward "conflicting claims to the division of social advantages" (Rawls). The just distribution of burdens and benefits certainly does'nt presuppose comparable powers or resources; what it seems to be inseparable from is a confrontation of different "ends and purposes" (Rawls) in respect of the same primary goods — with whatever initial chances for either side[167]. The interesting point however is that the perception of some situation as a conflict calling for a just solution is often generated by the choice of a perspective of justice itself. The repeal of apartheid may have come faster because of the fear of growing violence; but I think it would be wrong to underestimate the independent role played by a change in moral perception. Hume's fable characteristically ignores this counterfactual dimension: its very questionable lesson is that there can be no "restraint of justice" (as opposed to mere "laws of humanity") where no actual conflict of forces has arisen, the solution of which is advantageous to all parties. This shuts out a whole category of common discourse about the just and the unjust, which has to do with recognizing certain categories of persons as members of the moral community (eg.the manifold struggles for emancipation) and with enabling them to put forward claims at all (eg.legislation on worker's rights).

Now justice in respect of future generations surely demonstrates the independent role of such a moral perception to the highest degree. There is not, in that particular context, the least intimation of conflict as an observable feature of social life. The perception of a conflict between the interests of the living and the interests of future people depends on recognizing in the first place that future people have legitimate interests in the same finite resources. In other words: no such conflict would exist at all unless the planet's finite resources were not seen in the first place as resources held in common by the present and the future populations of the earth. Insofar, conflict is a normative construct.

---

[166] Bergson 1955 (1932), 68-70, 71.

[167] Barry 1989, 160: "(Where) there is extreme inequality of power, there may well still be a conflict of wants between the parties".

CHAPTER 5

JUSTICE IN CONTEXT:

THE VIEW FROM THE PRESENT

"Our concern with the future is...a concern with now: how well our life at
present is proceeding depends on its relation to a projected future."[168]

5.1 INTRODUCTION

In his recent book on ecology and politics O'Neill points out that our
concern with the long-term future reflects the fundamental interest we have
in being able to put the meanings we live by within a framework that
extends beyond our own lives. He argues that

> "all protagonists in the philosophical debate about future generations assume
> that there is a special problem with respect to our obligations to future gene-
> rations which is that we can benefit or harm them but that they cannot benefit
> or harm us"[169].That assumption reflects "the modern loss of any sense of com-
> munity with generations outside of our own times"[170]. So obligations to future
> generations are treated by philosophers as "obligations to strangers which are
> generated from a purely impersonal perspective"[171].

---

[168] O'Neill 1993, 55.

[169] Ibid., 27.

[170] Ibid., 28. O'Neill continues by deploring the lack of "any sense of reciprocal action
or dialogue" with future generations. I wonder whether reciprocity is the right concept
to work with in this context. Our relations with future generations show a quite different
pattern than the relations between contemporaries, which the doctrine of circumstances
of justice plausibly centres on reciprocity. Moreover, room should be left for a defense
of intergenerational justice based on the total *lack* of a "balance of power" in the environmental context. It is the absence of reciprocity which forms the right point of
departure for that argument.

[171] Ibid., 28.

O'Neill mentions utilitarianism and modified versions of Rawls' theory of justice.

As I already explained at the beginning of my argument, and as I shall reaffirm at its end, I think the "purely impersonal perspective" coincides with the moral one, and must counter on the level of principle the arbitrary power we, the living, exercise over the living conditions of future people. Many additional reasons moreover support the claim that justice between generations is an indispensable paradigm (see 4.1).

What must be admitted however is that the postulate of justice has to be situated within a wider framework. It must be seen within context. Our relations with future generations show a more complex pattern than is suggested by a description of the one-sided power we exercise over the life chances of potential people. The image of the linear structure of time completely isolating generations from one another (except the absolute power held by the present over a nameless future) reflects a part of reality, it does'nt reflect the whole of it. It is a picture that is deficient when we consider the realm of social meanings and values. The idea of justice between generations must be ready to face the question of our *interest* in the welfare of future generations. Why should we be interested in having balanced power relations with them? It is true that the idea of justice has no intrinsic need for proof of such a particular interest (or so I shall claim); the "interest" it reflects itself is synonymous with the "desire to be able to justify our conduct in an impartial way" (Barry) which we may suppose (with Brian Barry and others) to be an "original principle" in human nature. Insofar, it suffices to be aware of the fact that future people belong to the class of human beings. But the "original principle" cannot guarantee its own psychological strength — that is, its actual force in our minds. Because of the remarkably ambitious character of its projection into the long-term future, it wants to be considered (here more than elsewhere) within the wider field of practical motivation. Does its forward-looking attitude find a support in other values — values that give a meaning to our collective future? Several recent authors have helped me to become aware of this background dimension of intergenerational justice[172].

The detached view, the view of justice, is no easy conquest. It is unstable, because we cannot imagine ourselves as not belonging to the living, taking a certain position in time, and considering future states of affairs with a greater

---

[172] I mention especially Achterberg 1990 and 1994 (201-207), Birnbacher 1988, de-Shalit 1995, Hilhorst 1987, Meyer 1997 and O'Neill 1993.

or lesser measure of concern. We saw, when considering the issue of time preference (4.3.2), that the present claims a priority it is difficult to refuse in practice; our position in time as living people represents a very primary form of existential subjectivity. The move towards justice between generations is a move we make as living individuals, pressing ourselves to direct our sympathies at a particularly remote category of human beings (we cannot see future people on TV). The moral "vision from nowhere" here is a very demanding one: it apprehends time as a succession of states of affairs or events none of which has a lesser claim on our attention than the other. Can it find allies within the world of values?

Or does concern for justice in respect to future people work in a sort of social void? Let me already give a few examples that argue for the contrary. We found a family and care for its continuity, we fight for a juster society, we contribute to the development of science, we enlarge the world's eternal fund of great poems. These actions cannot be squared with indifference in regard to conditions beyond our own life-time. Their intrinsic meaning does not tolerate it: they presuppose some confidence in future people recognizing and developing further the values one has committed oneself to. So dependence goes both ways. Future generations represent for us the future such as it enters into the present meaning of things. A picture centred exclusively on power relations misses the historical dimension of man. We need a better view of what it is that makes the future *worthwhile* for ourselves, in our capacity of historical beings.

From such a perspective, what we are concerned with when we want to secure equal opportunities for future generations is to make room for our own experience of the good, by giving it a future it cannot do without. Intergenerational justice takes on the character of an instrument for keeping open a sufficient spectrum of life options across time. This instrumental role makes it serve a wider aim than it has by itself. Let me explain this as follows. What justice says is: let us care for justice between the successive inhabitants of the planet. This implies a concern with the basic welfare of future people: in Rawlsian terminology, the environmental resources of the planet are first assumed to be primary goods. But I already noted, under the heading of macro-ethics (2.5), that justice does'nt say: let us take care that there *be* future people; the uninterrupted habitation of the planet is taken for granted. The moral point of view (as instanced by the search for justice) does'nt, by itself, require the *existence* of its constituency; so it is not capable of resisting a call for the collective suicide of humanity. This may be considered a quite fantastic eventuality. Now this I precisely what I want to suggest: that the difficulty in taking that extreme hypothesis seriously reveals an elemental (and therefore poorly articulated) assumption of the perpetuity of human life on the planet, which forms the horizon for our experience of the good across time. In striving for the equal opportunities of future generations, justice does more than serve its intrinsic distributive aim, it also supports the realization of a wider world of values. But can these values be made explicit?

5.1.1 Present time of entry. The future as our future

I already discussed Rawls' "present time of entry interpretation" of the original position, by relating it to the doctrine of the circumstances of justice (4.3.1). But I suggested at the same time that it might be explained in the first place (Rawls is'nt sufficiently clear on the subject) by the simple fact that the detached view cannot make us forget the situated one, or in other words, that it cannot let us ignore that we ("we" who actually *perform* the thought experiment called "original position") do belong to the living. The detached view is in a state of constant tension with the view from the present. Let me comment on that.

The original position

> "is not to be thought of as a general assembly which includes at one moment everyone who will live at some time; or, much less, as an assembly of everyone who could live at some time"[173].

This seems natural enough. If we consider the original position as a thought experiment which one must actually be capable of making in order to test the social arrangements of real life, it is impossible to let the veil of ignorance fall over that very primal piece of knowledge which consists in being aware of being alive i.e. of belonging to the living generation. I think there is a qualitative difference here with trying to separate oneself in one's imagination from circumstances such as one's position in society, one's relative position within a process of historical development etc. Past, present and future cannot be robbed of their existential specificity. In other words, the original position, which symbolizes through the veil of ignorance a stipulated exchangeability of persons, and which does extend the latter to one's position in history (one does'nt know what the relative position of one's generation is in terms of economic or cultural progress) cannot be used to symbolize impartiality as

---

[173] Rawls 1971, 139.

between persons distinguished on the basis of their belonging either to the living or to the concourse of past or potential (future) persons. It is impossible to imagine ourselves actually changing places with past or future people. So any definition of the original position has to keep us aware of the existential fact of being alive; justice in respect of future generations is inevitably a move we make towards a future contemplated from the always unique position we have in the here and now. There is no plausible way to carry out a thought experiment projecting us into an undifferentiated co-presence of past, present and future.

For we live within time, between the past and the future (the detached view cannot free us from that ineradicable reality of time: its irreversible flow); the terms of "past" and "future" are meaningless unless related to a certain position in time (the detached view cannot acknowledge on its own any existential difference between the two); so the expression of "future generations" does'nt come alive unless that position in time we call "the present" is presupposed in its full existential force.

Let us be clear about this. Our objectifying impulse (Nagel) is strong enough to let us imagine a detached position, from which we consider our own place in history as a contingent one. That is the point of view which inspires Rawls' conceptual scheme in the first place, with its intergenerational cooperation and related notion of just savings. It also can be illustrated by the forms of justice I mentioned in 4.2 above: they schematize relations over time in a general, non-situated sense, the position of actuality (of belonging to the living) being occupied successively by the one generation after the other. When we choose that detached point of view, we don't identify with any particular generation. But that detachment is arrived at against the background of a constant awareness of existential actuality: there is no way in which we could imagine ourselves *to be* past or potential persons. The experience of being is an experience of actuality, of the present, as distinguished from past and future.

So I have the greatest difficulty with authors who declare it not be counter-intuitive to imagine, as concerns the parties to the original position, that they don't know whether they belong to the current generation, and so must consider the risk of turning out to be (!) a future generation — or who even endow those parties with the faculty of considering themselves as "possibly existing" individuals who realize that they have (!) an interest in being actually existent[174].

One might argue that there is some artificiality in allowing people to know that they belong to the living while banning knowledge of their position in history. Can one dissociate the second sort of knowledge from the first one? I think the answer must be that there does'nt seem to be any greater intrinsic difficulty in stipulating ignorance of one's position in history than ignorance in respect of other important aspects of one's individual identity such as one's personal talents, one's personal status within society etc. (nobody pretends that it is easy to take the detached view), whereas "detachment" is a quite implausible move in relation to one's existential actuality. Stressing the latter point then offers a sufficient basis for developing an argument that centres on the situated view.

We cannot exchange places with future people: that existential non-exchangeability is replicated by the circumstance that we live together with other people who are our contemporaries, and that we don't do so with future people. Whatever counterfactual power we may actually allow to the idea of justice, it still is an occasion for wonder that our intuitions let that power develop in respect of people we can have no business with (people which moral concern can only make us "see" in their abstract quality of potential human beings, full stop).

5.1.2 Justice and the step beyond coexistence

I have argued that Rawls' "circumstances of justice" are counter-intuitive because they make it impossible to account for the equalizing potential of the idea of justice. This potential finds an application in intergenerational equity. The knowledge that we are dealing with human beings who must share basic resources with us while being at our mercy works as a strong enough motive for securing to them, in moral terms, an equal position which they entirely miss at the empirical level.

However, I think that a full explanation of justice to future generations calls for some further explorations in moral theory. What I mean is that even when the socially corrective power of justice has been admitted in a general sense (against Hume), the realization that we cannot change places with past and future sharpens awareness of how peculiar it is that our sense of justice lets that corrective power reach beyond the limits of society, understood as a

---

[174] Singer 1988, 221; Norton 1989, 150.

presently existing entity. It is an ancient wisdom that justice has the vocation of organizing the coexistence between individuals. According to Kant, justice rules the conditions under which my freedom can be made to agree with yours; what we now need to wonder about is that justice to future generations is made to govern the conditions under which the freedom of living people can be made to agree with the freedom of merely potential ones. No coexistence does of course exist with these people; the material "intercourse" we have with them is a unilateral one: we do, or don't leave them enough to stay alive (we do, or don't put time bombs in their midst). Nevertheless, our sense of justice here intervenes and shapes normative structures that bridge distance in time and so abandon reciprocity.

Let me elaborate somewhat more on the question whether there is a non-contingent relation between the idea of justice and a context of people living as contemporaries.

Has the notion of people living together as contemporaries been made irrelevant by criticism levelled at the circumstances of justice? I don't think so: it only has in the sense of people dealing with one another on terms of equal bargaining power, it has'nt in the more general and rather trivial sense of society being "a cooperative venture for mutual advantage...typically marked by a conflict as well as an identity of interests" (Rawls). Justice normally rules an interactive pattern between individuals who "coexist together at the same time on a definite geographical territory"[175].

Our readiness to criticize Hume's fable and to ask for a "restraint of justice" in respect of the inferior creatures he imagines (they can never make us "feel the effects of their resentment") surely is related to the circumstance that Hume imagines these creatures to be "intermingled with men", and men to have "intercourse" with them (although Hume does'nt want to call such intercourse a "society"). Let us assume that the existence of intelligent creatures on the planet Saturn has been proved by long-distance space photography, that no contacts of any sort have been established with these creatures (nor will be within a foreseeable future), and that a risk of harming

---

[175] Rawls 1971, 126. "Mutual advantage" in the former passage must probably be interpreted in a more flexible way than when its meaning is defined by association with Hume's circumstances of justice. Cf.also Rawls 1993, 17: what people "gain" from a well-ordered society is first of all that they live in a mutual relation of reciprocity which expresses a "public political conception of justice". So equality comes first: with the difference principle, "everyone benefits judged with respect to an appropriate benchmark of equality" (see also Rawls 1971, 103).

their environment would exist if humans were to send an unmanned space capsule to Saturn. Would we say that it would be unjust to launch that capsule anyway? Would'nt we rather say, less pointedly, that it would be wrong, our explanation of this moral criticism not being framed in terms of (in)justice, but simply in terms of a natural duty not to harm or injure another?

I said that justice between generations demonstrates the potential for correcting situations of inequality that inheres in the concept of justice. But it should be remarked that the deeper ratio of this corrective power can be explained in ways that relate it very much to situations of coexistence. Let me recall the interpretation of the golden rule as a norm of mutual recognition applied to circumstances characterized by social asymmetry. Justice at work between people living together and aiming at a basic equality in their mutual relations[176]. For instance, it is a purpose of many forms of social legislation to develop the opportunities for effective partnership (political, social, cultural) of certain categories of citizens. Partnership as "taking part", on a basis of mutual recognition, cooperation and exchange: reciprocity as a state of affairs to be wished for, as a condition of community. Insofar, the interactive context of people living at the same time and on the same territory would seem to be very important for understanding what justice is about.

Rawls himself develops a *normative* concept of reciprocity that provides a basic criterion for the quality of social relations and that is quite different from the *empirical* notion of reciprocity underlying the circumstances of justice. It expresses an idea of mutual benefit which naturally presupposes coexistence.

> "Being governed by (the principles of justice) means that we want to live with others on terms that everyone would recognize as fair from a perspective that all would accept as reasonable."[177]

"To live with others": it is clear that we need to suppose people living as contemporaries on the same territory and forming social entities of some sort. It must be remarked here that the whole Rawlsian explanation of the stability of conceptions of justice also develops within a context of implied reciprocity. Rawls emphasizes that the principles of moral psychology which underpin the growth of a sense of justice within a well-ordered society (i.e. engender in human beings the desire to act upon a conception of justice) are "reciprocity

---

[176] Cf.Walzer 1983, 65 and 81-82 on the common life being a normative, counter-factual construct. Every serious effort at communal provision is redistributive in character.

[177] Rawls 1971, 478.

principles"[178]. Ties of friendship and fellow feeling, and concern for the approbation of the wider society, at first play a crucial role; becoming attached to the highest order principles themselves depends on

> "the recognition that we and those for whom we care are the beneficiaries of an established and enduring just institution...In due course we come to appreciate the ideal of just human cooperation."[179]

So the acquisition of a sense of justice is continuous with our "natural sentiments": it rests upon attachments to particular persons and groups, and upon a desire to advance human interests, which naturally evoke the fullness of social life as we live it by interacting with others.

***

I have argued that even when one feels justified to claim (against Hume) that justice has a counterfactual power in a general sense (a claim which makes one reject Rawls' circumstances of justice), the realization that it is nonsense to imagine oneself actually changing places with people located in the past or in the future (i.e. that it is impossible to carry out in that particular case the mental operation called for by reciprocity in its normative aspect) must sharpen one's awareness of the ambitious character of intergenerational justice. I said that it is an ancient wisdom that justice has the vocation of organizing the coexistence between individuals, and I mentioned Rawls' claim that "(being) governed by (the principles of justice) means that we want to live with others on terms that everyone would recognize as fair" (putting myself special emphasis on the words "live with others"). One cannot avoid seeing a stark contrast between justice fulfilling its task of a right distribution of "the common stock and the incidents of communal enterprise"[180] in the midst of the "thick" and living reality of

---

[178] Ibid., 453 (see also 177, 455). Ibid. 499: the sense of justice corresponding to justice as fairness is stronger than the parallel sentiment inculcated by other conceptions, because the effect of the concerns embodied in justice as fairness "is to heighten the operation of the reciprocity principle". The moral psychology developed in Rawls 1971 is left unchanged by Rawls 1993 (cf.142-143), but completed by a (strongly normative) account of "reason" and of the "rational" which is less relevant for our own purposes.

[179] Ibid., 473-474. These views are developed in 473-477. Cf.also Rawls 1993, 315f.

[180] Finnis 1980, 166. The notion of justice relating to the distribution of a "common stock" is an evident help to explaining intergenerational justice in the environmental

contemporary social life, and its operation within the new and in a sense abstract realm of our relations with future generations, towards regions of time and conditions of life we can scarcely imagine.

Now what is plain is that in spite of everything that has been said above, the vocation of justice to organize coexistence, although most important of course, is no exclusive one. For we do have an intuitive conception of justice between generations, which lets us seek for a right distribution of environmental resources between ourselves, the living, and beings whose existence is a merely potential one. Is this a fact which just has to be taken for granted, in spite of the peculiar character which it shows on reflection? One might argue that there is nothing peculiar in moral concern being extended to all human beings, wherever situated in space or time. I agree with that, but I feel that our recourse to the concept of justice beyond the limits of coexistence still calls for some sort of special explanation, even when the counterfactual power of justice has been conceded in a general way. Do future generations appear to us in exactly the same guise as do contemporary victims of ecological exploitation?

Let me observe first of all that the temporal dimension creates no strictly conceptual obstacles to seeing ourselves engaged with future people in the sort of situation which calls for the intervention of distributive justice (considering the fact that we do conceive justice between generations, it would be surprising if such obstacles did exist). The notion that we have to share a common source of life is sustained by a sense of common identity in the following sense: when discussing the concept of future generations, I remarked that the gradual way in which the individuals composing the family, the group, the nation, or mankind at large are replaced, allows us to imagine ourselves as being members, with future generations, of one processional entity. Another natural element of understanding is offered by the camping ground analogy and its background paradigm of "leaving enough for the next man". Justice finds an expression in the vocabulary of temporal succession.

No strictly conceptual obstacles block the way towards intergenerational justice. The strangeness of the notion rather derives from its apparent *lack of social context*. One gets the impression that in being put at work beyond the limits of coexistence, the concept of justice is forced to operate in a void, beyond the reach of a whole mode of discourse which puts the concept at the

---

sphere (as is Rawls' more general notion of "primary goods"); the challenge rather lies in making room for the notion of "communal enterprise"!

centre of the just society and relates it to the wider world of the moral, social and psychological aspects of human community. For instance, I observed that Rawls defines the just society in terms of how people live together, by putting a normative conception of reciprocity at the centre of his whole conception of justice as fairness. This conception fits the explanation of justice within a wider framework of moral psychology, thus relating its reality as a motive to considerations turning on the sustaining virtues or on our natural sentiments, which all presuppose a situation of people living as contemporaries.

What I am working towards is the idea that there is more to our subject than a problem of "extending" justice as fairness to cover our duties to future generations, as Rawls formulates it[181]. One must presume that there are ways of understanding the affirmation of justice to future generations within a wider context of values and interests. Values and interests that orient us towards the future and which take the place of that social "fullness of life" which surrounds justice between contemporaries.

Rawls himself takes a step in that direction with his motivational assumption: a step which remains very timid because it does'nt cross the conceptual limits imposed by his circumstances of justice. What is much more important is the reason why he puts justice to future generations on his agenda in the first place: he considers society as a cooperative venture over time. The life of a people is conceived as a scheme of cooperation spread out in historical time, whose purpose is to realize and preserve a just society by means of a principle of just savings. In other words, justice is tied to society as a historical reality. Let us be precise: Rawls makes it clear enough that he considers justice over time to stand on its own feet (as is confirmed by his rejection of time preference); but the *occasion* for doing so introduces a dimension that cannot be accounted for by a general commitment to impartiality. Through the scheme of cooperation, society is launched into the dimension of time; the just savings principle follows from recognizing (in a particularly teleological form) the historical dimension of man.

STRANGERS?

The contrast between justice as the organizing concept of a living society and justice as a norm applied within the dimension of time might suggest that future people have a moral position comparable to that of strangers. I think this suggestion is wrong, for the following reasons.

---

[181] Rawls 1993, 21.

Rawls' theory evidently equates society with the national community and the pre-eminent powers it has for establishing, within its borders, a just order of things. Let me only mention, in this respect, the demand made by the concept of justice on the capacity of organized communities to shape law-making or judicial institutions, and to take care of enforcement requirements (how could Rawls' difference principle become an operational one without the taxation apparatus of the modern state?). So for Rawls, the law of nations forms a special problem. Now, taking account of the identification of "society" with "national state", let us consider ourselves to be citizens of a particular state and imagine a category of people ("strangers"), with whom no cooperative arrangements exist such as they exist between ourselves and the other citizens of our country. According to Rawls, the moral terrain we are then walking upon lies outside justice as fairness: our behavior is regulated by natural duties of mutual aid holding between persons irrespective of their institutional relationships. For instance, there is a duty to help another when he is in need, provided that one can do so without excessive risk or loss to oneself; there is the duty not to harm or injure another, etc.[182]

Now any closer look reveals the serious defects of a comparison of future people with a category of people defined as strangers in the way I just mentioned.

To begin with, it is justice and not a vague duty to help or not to harm that fits our intuitions in respect of future generations (see 4.1). The international community understands our duties to them as implying a notion of equality over time. Vague duties offer no clear moral basis for the sustainable society.

Second, putting future people on the same level as beings with whom we only have chance encounters is difficult to reconcile with our natural understanding of generational renewal. The latter is perceived as affecting *one* enduring entity (family, group, nation, mankind), future people thus participating, with us, in a common processional reality. There is an elemental idea of society going on. This perception is, in a sense, an empty (purely formal) one, but it suggests concerns that give it a substantive content.

Third, the premise itself of identifying "society" with the national state is doubtful enough, even when corrected in some ways by a law of nations in the (very minimalist) Rawlsian style. Although it is true that we must turn to

---

[182] Rawls 1971, 115. See also Walzer 1983, 33: "It is the absence of any cooperative arrangements that sets the context for mutual aid". Although he agrees with Rawls in stipulating a duty of positive assistance in case of urgent need, Walzer thinks that what strangers owe one another "is by no means clear".

national communities in order to find entities that pretend to provide the full panoply of just arrangements between individuals, we live in a period of history where justice on a world-wide scale has become a living issue. The central message of Rawls' first principle of justice (the "equal basic liberties") already works between nations on the aspirational level since 1948 (UN Declaration on Human Rights). Moreover, modern states have not waited on this declaration to let aliens share the basic freedoms stipulated in their constitutions. Is there still room in the present world for a clear distinction between citizens to whom justice is owed, and "strangers" having no call on us except "mutual aid"? The continuous growth of economic relations between countries (or rather: between economic power centres that short-circuit the national state), the tremendous increase in travel and communication facilities, the development of humanitarian assistance on an international scale, and last but not least the global character of our main environmental concerns, shape a nascent world society where the stranger is becoming a co-citizen in important respects.

5.1.3 Moral reason and moral motivation

It is because of the morally novel and exacting character of concern for the long-term that the theorist needs to ask with some insistence what makes the future live for us as a dimension of moral responsibility. Can the weight of caring for intergenerational justice be borne solely by a lofty respect for moral impartiality? Must we not presume that trust in an open future has a substantive meaning for us? Through articulating that side of our experience the theorist can perhaps help to strengthen our forward-looking attitudes. The appeal for an impartial treatment of future generations must surely depend in part, for its effectiveness, on ourselves first becoming conscious of our investment in an open temporal horizon.

Let me repeat that I have no intention of grounding intergenerational justice on sentiments (e.g. on a feeling of solidarity with future generations). I prefer to base my argument on the Kantian view that moral rules may not be made to depend on the whims of sentiment. Morality must show its force where sentiment cannot be relied upon. That view is particularly apt in our context of discussion, as we must contemplate the ecological plight of potential persons we know nothing about. So I concur with writers like Barry, Birnbacher, Nagel or Rawls, who all defend the general position that the moral point of view, the detached view that is aimed at by the "objectifying impulse" of ethics ("..."the basic insight that appears from the impersonal standpoint is that everyone's life matters, and no one is more important than anyone else"[183]) generates an independent reason for action i.e. a motivational factor in its own right[184]. As Rawls formulates it,

> "the force, or weight, of principle-dependent desires is given entirely by the principle to which the desire is attached, and not by the psychological strength of the desire itself"[185].

But when this premise has been firmly put into place, nothing hinders us from questioning the conditions under which its psychological strength is maximized. The need for a motivational support of the moral point of view in its orientation towards the future is demonstrated by any closer study of the facts. Moral reason must fight against psychological limitations that strongly limit its actual chances. Our intuitions (however noble) are too often unsuccessful in governing our actual attitudes. Contemporary political life shows that the will to translate ecological aims with a wide scientific backing into effective policies is anything but self-evident (this even applies to aims which condition the expectations of our direct descendants). So let us pay attention to the actual context! Distance in time has a stronger psychological impact than distance in space because it implies the non-actuality of relevant states of affairs, and even (beyond a certain range) the non-existence and thus the invisibility of the people one is concerned with. Non-actuality explains the widespread economic practice of discounting future values (a general preference for short-term values is built into the market economy itself); as to mere potentiality, it creates an extreme form of anonymity and it also entails a

---

[183] Nagel 1991, 11.

[184] Cf.Nagel 1986, 151, on purely rational motivation. See also Rawls 1993, 49 note 2: Rawls agrees with Scanlon "that we have a basic desire to be able to justify our actions to others on grounds they could not reasonably reject". This links up with the *idea* of reciprocity: 50. Cf.also 82f on "principle-dependent desires". So when Rawls develops the idea that justice as fairness "is continuous with our natural sentiments" (Rawls 1971, 477) this should not be interpreted in the sense of a derivation from psychological data. Cf.also Rawls 1993, 71 on the educative role played by justice as fairness itself.- Discussing an argument that although we do not have obligations *to* future generations, we may have obligations of fair play among contemporaries *with respect* to future generations (the hypothesis is that nearly all of us are concerned to a certain extent with their welfare), Brian Barry remarks that such a derivative obligation among ourselves, which is entirely parasitic upon our actual sentiments, cannot generate the conclusion that we *should* care for their welfare: Barry 1979, 72.

[185] Rawls 1993, 82 note 31.

complete absence of reciprocity: the living generation can dictate living conditions to future generations without having to fear reprisals. Finally, environmental hazards tend to have a global scope that force us to think in the
still unusual terms of the future interests of humanity at large. It is an essential
aspect of our subject that moral concern must extend to human beings living
beyond the usual reach of our sympathies (and certainly enjoying no
bargaining position of any sort!).

I already discussed the psychological aspect within the context or rejecting
time preference and I cited Glover on "moral distance" (4.3.2). I considered
Nagel's view that the emotional attitudes condemned by the rationalist may
reflect in certain cases moral reasons which compete with the detached
position and so create a split within the domain of ethics (Nagel mentions —
tentatively, it is true — the "claim of immediacy"). So there is an at least
potential menace to the hegemony of the detached position (the position I
identified with the moral point of view). I suggested that two avenues exist for
restoring moral harmony in favour of the detached position, the position of
justice: critical discussion, and more realistically, politics. The avenue I am
suggesting at the present stage is, somewhat paradoxically, a psychological
one: fighting against our psychological limitations by articulating those
elements in the world of living values which orientate us towards the future.
Within the sphere of our relations with future generations, "psychology" does
not only *limit* the chances of rational belief: it may sometimes *improve* them,
by countering bias with substantive motives that make us care for the welfare
of future people. Justice surely finds a welcome support in those aspects of our
moral life which fight the power of short-term interests by giving to future
generations a greater visibility, thus setting the stage for the full operation of
our moral beliefs. Looking for such support is a moral duty by itself once the
premise of justice between generations has been firmly locked into position:
there is no serious commitment to a moral principle which does'nt care for its
effective application. I think it is possible to apply here what Jonas says within
the more general (macro-ethical) framework of his "ethics of the future": the
imagined fate of future men does not of itself have the influence it ought to
have upon our feeling — so we should purposely make room for it in our
minds. We must "educate our soul" to a willingness to let itself be affected[186].
Nagel says something like this about ethics in general:

---

[186] Jonas 1984, 28.

"If we are required to do certain things, then we are required to be the kinds of people who will do those things."[187]

5.2 VALUES ACROSS GENERATIONS

What values are at stake when our common future is endangered by environmental harm?

I sometimes feel there is an essential obscurity to the subject that even discourages its tentative exploration, or forces it too soon into unmanageable metaphysics. Our powers for environmental destruction compel us to accept moral responsibility within an unprecedented time frame; if values exist which cause us to consider our common future at such a wider range, they are poorly articulated; there is no guarantee that we have anything in hand except the general commitment to a universalist morality.

I suggested that there is a natural understanding of society as on ongoing reality, and that it is on the basis of such a natural understanding of generational succession that we can ask what substantive forward-looking concerns enter into the wish for intergenerational justice. But we can't know at first how far this is going to get us. Try facing people with a fictional forecast that the survival of humanity or at least the preservation of a material basis for civilization (life becoming "brutish, nasty and short") is going to be threatened within some few hundred years, and that it is up to us all to do something about it. And ask them whether they care, and if so, why. The chances are that they will become the victim of a mental cramp. Answers will not come forward easily.

Let me start with the philosophical platitude which already was at the background of the "present time of entry" issue (see 5.1.1). Man is a being that lives in time, whose life indeed is temporal through and through, and for whom the future consequently is a constitutive dimension of his existence, as much as his remembrance of the past. Every time that we position ourselves in time by saying "now", we already find ourselves on the way towards the next minute, the next day, the next year. It is no exaggeration to say that we *are* in time, that our being is a being-in-time, positioned between past and future. That being-in-time is not an object of will, but an ontological dimension of our existence, which conditions the exercise of will itself; something that is

---

[187] Nagel 1986, 191.

already there as an essential structure of human existence. I here consider "existence" to extend as well to social life: we live in time together, and so take part in that collective being-in-time we call "history".

Of course this is no more than the outline of a basic characteristic of existence, of a mode of being; I gain a less abstract level by asking how we actually let that mode of being *come alive*, how we let it enter the world of motives. I said there is a natural understanding of society as on ongoing reality; the search for continuity is woven in a self-evident way into most of our social practices and institutions, or even characterizes their inner meaning. Let me mention (inter alia) the family, education, saving (investment), legal regulation, the pursuit of political stability, or the conservation of monuments and other artistic products. Because of the pervasive presence of time, its very being is for society equivalent to surviving, caring for things going on. I cite Michael Walzer on education:

> "Every human society educates its children, its new and future members. Education expresses what is, perhaps, our deepest wish: to continue, to go on, to persist in the face of time. It is a program for social survival."[188]

The search for perpetuity build upon an implicit confidence in constant generational renewal: the practices and institutions that maintain it are meant to be taken over, so long-run continuity is as it were shining through, it magnetizes the whole process without being the directly contemplated goal itself. As Richard Epstein formulates it in an interesting argument:

> "(in) general, if we continue to create sound institutions for the present, then the problem of future generations will pretty much take care of itself, even if we do not develop overarching policies of taxation or investment that target future generations for special consideration."[189]

Epstein's argument mentions many different factors that contribute to the complex fabric of social continuity: the strong psychological continuity of individuals over time, the natural bequest motive in the relations between parents and children, the new generation's own set of endowments, the permanence of physical assets, or the continuous transmission of humanity's stock of knowledge.

It is the next step that keeps us busy, so to speak. But that is so, says Epstein, if we continue to create sound institutions for the present — the

---

[188] Walzer 1983, 197.

[189] Epstein 1992, 85.

concept of "institution" introducing, by definition, an implicit claim on ordering things in a durable way. In his "Imperative of responsibility" Hans Jonas describes traditional modes of future-oriented ethics, and within that framework, he offers a short phenomenology of institutional life. The wisdom of the statesman consists in the wisdom he devotes to the present.

> "The best state, so it was thought, is also the best for the future, precisely because the stable equilibrium of its present ensures its future as such ... . Duration results as a concomitant of what is good now and at all times."[190]

I think that this description, though it is directed at premodern societies in the first place, still broadly fits contemporary life (although the words "good...at all times" might perhaps receive nowadays a sceptical response).

What is new in the present situation is that because of the impact of our economy and technology on the environment, we have to accept responsibility for the life chances of future generations, these chances thus having *to be faced directly*, within a time-span (or in response to a degree of risk)[191] which divorces that responsibility from the standard forms and conditions of social continuity (Epstein admits in the article I just cited from that the environment may need the longer view). A typical instance is provided by the time-bomb effect. The issue of protection against radioactive fall-out confronts us with future generations living at very remote periods; one has to take measures capable of being effective over a quasi indefinite length of time. Sacrifices may have to be asked for on behalf of a very distant future indeed. I observe, by way of contrast, that the direct foresight involved in such important fields of decision-making as parental care, economics or politics does'nt seem to reach very much beyond a period of some 20 to 50 years (I may be too optimistic).

Does that mean that we are outdistancing all the substantive concerns that go into maintaining society as an ongoing proposition, and that we must keep satisfied with the independent strength of a universalist morality? In other words, is the motivational fabric of social continuity capable of coping with the new scale of human enterprise?

---

[190] Jonas 1984, 15.

[191] The issue of global warming is an example: serious effects of global warming may already occur within a relatively short period of, say, 50 years, but then it is the possible degree of global disruption, and the need to prevent it by structural changes in our economy, which gives it an unprecedented dimension.

I already suggested that the search for continuity builds upon an implicit confidence in constant generational renewal. Perpetuity is aimed at in an indirect and implicit way, through the practices and patterns that secure continuity within a more or less limited range ("the children shall take over"). For our usual patterns of action, the more distant future forms a horizon which remains outside our centre of vision (we cannot focus upon it), although an apocalyptic forecast concerning it would probably affect us with strongly negative feelings. I think such a forecast (should we really internalize it) would reveal an implicit trust in the future of mankind as an indefinitely open one, whatever a more detached point of view might tell us about the transience of all human affairs, or about the sun getting cold within some millions of years. That trust always stays at the receding edge of our vision: it finds few words, unless we are prepared to speculate about it at some deep level of philosophical or religious reflection. Why do we want human life and culture to go on? The question is, in what sense we can be said to "want" it.

I shall remark in section 5.3 on the challenge this presents to philosophy. The subject perhaps touches upon a dimension of existence which is structurally resistant to any giving of reasons. The rationalist might be tempted to deny the finality of that resistance; he would say that in the end, what our collective future represents for us *is* the whole of reasons we have for wishing the world to go on (though he may admit that many of those reasons are difficult to unearth). For instance, he may be of the opinion that what we trust in is the possibility of progressing together towards a better state of humanity. I myself doubt whether *reasons* can bear the full weight of our confidence in an open horizon for mankind. I think a more plausible view on the matter is that this confidence forms a background dimension on which values (and particularly values with a long-term aspect) necessarily *depend* in order to stay alive, grow, and renew themselves. Dante gives us a clue in his Inferno:

"Therefore thou mayest understand that all our knowledge shall be dead, from that moment when the portal of the Future shall be closed"[192].

So the question is, whether that fundamental orientation on the perpetuity of mankind, though forming in a sense an inexhaustible background which defies rational analysis, does'nt yet find an *embodiment* in identifiable values that can be shown to have, intrinsically, a wider temporal reach than the "daily" concerns that sustain short-run continuity. Values that either lay a

---

[192] Dante 1904, Canto X p.107.

claim to an indefinitely open-ended time horizon, or target future generations within a more or less definite time-span, although they are served in the normal run of affairs by the practices and patterns that maintain social continuity — so that their intergenerational span only becomes quite manifest when the goods they are related to are threatened, by developments in a more distant future. It is when action has to be taken to save them that these goods become an object of will and thus enter the world of motives.

I think such values can indeed be identified. We find on closer inspection that the commitment to certain values we can give a name to carries us beyond our own life-time: values that are capable of putting remote periods or even an indefinitely open future at the centre of our vision. They give a concrete shape to the longer view. Let me recall my fictional forecast that the survival of humanity or at least the preservation of a material basis for civilization is going to be threatened within some hundred years, and that it is up to us all to do something about it. I suggested that if people were asked whether they care, and if so, why, they would probably become the victim of a mental cramp. I now want to suggest that after having given some thought to the matter, they might possibly come forward with specific reasons for action. They would say for instance that they identify with the fate of their (great)-grand-children. They would have got a clearer view on the future beyond their own life-time by articulating personal attachments. As John Passmore formulates it in his book on ecology,

"to love...is to care about the future of what we love"[193].

They might also realize that what the future holds in store is the absurd end of long-term projects they are contributing to with others.

"When men act for the sake of the future they will not live to see, it is for the most part out of love for persons, places and forms of activity..."

"Forms of activity" applies to this more transpersonal element, it opens onto human endeavour in all its forms[194]. Passmore's formulation at the same time expresses the concrete character of the motives for action one can expect

---

[193] Passmore 1974, 88.

[194] Ibid., 89. Note that such a more transpersonal element may already be at work in somebody's concern with the fate of his (great-)grand-children: it is not only their personal life expectations that are under threat, it also is (even more certainly) the future beyond *their* own life-time, which *they* are interested in.

to exist. The future is seen as it were through particular goods. As Hume says
it,

> "there is no such passion in human minds as the love of mankind, merely as
> such, independent of personal qualities, of services or of relation to our-
> self"[195].

There is at least something improbable in people being moved by the pallid
idea of the future of mankind, although *that* is a motive to which the
ecological world situation should let us "educate our souls" (Jonas) already!

I mentioned Passmore's "love of persons, places and forms of activity" in
order to illustrate long-term values. Other concepts are also helpful: consider
for instance the notion of an "institution". I quoted Epstein and Jonas on good
institutions securing the conditions of durability by a good ordering of the
present social state of affairs. That ordering makes an implicit claim to an
ongoing validity. Constitutions provide a clear example. They are
"constitutions" insofar as they raise certain values (for instance the separation
of powers, fundamental rights, the rule of law) above the normal run of
political affairs; one cannot imagine one's community not adhering to them.
Those values are held to "constitute" political life and so to have a natural
claim on durability. One expects such goods "to have a future", just as one
also does with great monuments or works of art.

***

The basic issue here is one of articulation. In his "Sources of the self",
Charles Taylor says that we find the sense of life through articulating it and
thus relating it to a greater pattern[196]. He criticizes contemporary philosophy
for turning a blind eye to questions about what makes our lives meaningful
or fulfilling; an involvement with the past and the future, on an intergenerational scale, characterizes many of those "inescapable frameworks of
meaning" that give a spiritual orientation to our lives. He even affirms that
the goods we assume and draw on in any claim to rightness "only exist for

---

[195] Hume, A treatise of human nature, book 3, part 2, section 1. A more inspiring view
is to be found in Henri Bergson, Les deux sources de la morale et de la religion, Paris
1932 (ed.PUF 1955, p.68): according to Bergson, we are moving from a "morale
close" to a "morale ouverte".

[196] Taylor 1989, 18

us through *some* articulation"[197]. I refer to his extensive and illuminating treatment of the subject.

I immediately add that Taylor strongly underlines the difficulty of such an articulation. Now that difficulty is a still greater one in our case, because the visibility of meanings that relate us to future generations depends upon rejecting certain philosophical positions that are widely held today. I think O'Neill (1993) is right in thinking that the identification of value presupposes a philosophical framework that accomodates qualitative ("perfectionist") elements that transcend the mere factum of individual preference and allow a discussion on the good life. So subjectivist positions let us walk blindfolded. Another obstacle lies in liberal individualism, although one can find allies against it in the different representatives of the so-called communitarian school of thought: the meanings that link us with future generations are eminently shared meanings, they reflect values that fashion the communities we live in. The further we look forward in time, the more our images of the future are shaped by our shared aspirations and common purposes rather than by our individual wants and utilities.

5.2.1 Aspects of intergenerational value

The question how our values can commit us to the longer view, and cause us to have a direct interest in states of affairs beyond our own life-time, is an extremely wide-ranging one. It is related to many aspects of life and strongly dependent on the historical and cultural context. So I shall limit my discussion to some philosophical issues of a general kind that seem to determine the background structure of intergenerational value. The latter topic is, in fact, a philosophically very provocative one; the sort of experience it refers to finds no place in our understanding of man and society unless certain avenues in philosophical thought are chosen and others rejected. I now give a short list of the issues in question.

(i) Concern with the welfare of future generations first raises an issue for our understanding of the self. It draws attention to all ways in which the constitution of the self depends on the self transcending the limits of its empirical life-form, through love, commitment and community.

(ii) Self-transcendence implies perceiving future people as those who will enjoy (or participate in the enjoyment of) the values we are committed to, and

---

[197] Ibid., 91 (curs.in the text). Ibid.: "...articulation is a necessary condition of adhesion: without it, these goods are not even options".

whom we expect to further their realization. So it would be impossible to ignore the concept of intergenerational cooperation at this stage.

(iii) The scope for intergenerational value surely is affected, in our contemporary culture, by that culture's sensitivity to historical change. What confidence do we allow ourselves in the permanent validity of the goods upon which we orientate our actions? Any account of intergenerational commitment must face the challenge of modern historical relativism, such as it is rooted itself in the experience of rapid social transformation. It is the same dynamics of technology and of the economy that let us walk the brink of "ecospace", that foster a multiple break with tradition, and that make it impossible to foresee what the future will bring. The topic, evidently, is a vast one, and the present argument can do no more than remark on some central points. Does the notion of timeless value still have any reality for us? Is it rather progress — a sense of direction — which forms, for modern man, the inevitable mode of mastering the transience of things? Or does contemporary culture close off any avenue towards solidarity with future generations because of its being dominated by the short-term forces of the market and by the unforeseeable developments of technology? In short: can anything be said, in a general way, about the manner in which contemporary culture structures social time i.e. relates itself to the past and the future, or is our collective experience of time perhaps a multi-layered and fragmented one?

(iv) As it is a condition of many experiences of the good that we may be able to expect its future validity and further development within a time-frame that extends beyond our own lives, the claim is a plausible one that measures which justify trust in the long-term future serve a public good — the good of living in a society that has the character of being open to the future. This can be considered, itself, to belong to the just basic structure discussed in the previous chapter. Let me explain this as follows. Justice wants us to care, on a basis of impartiality across time, for the ecological conditions of an equal worth of liberty. It is supported, in requiring us to do so, by our desire to trust in the long-term future, for it is on that trust that the chances for many important values depend. Now what this amounts to is that we see justice serve, through its concern for an equal *worth* of liberty, that important element of a *meaningful* liberty which consists in being able to choose among a wide spectrum of goods, many of which carry us beyond our own span of life. At the same time, the norm of justice makes it clear that this is not only a matter regarding ourselves (the living), but also something we must care for on behalf of future generations.

ON HAVING CHILDREN

It is a striking fact that the question, why people have children, lies at the core of our subject. The question may sound somewhat unusual; it is rarely posed, perhaps because there are either no answers or too many. But of course it has everything to do, in the most direct way, with creating for oneself an interest in things going on. We want our children to have a future: the interest is a personal one but it opens into an interest in all aspects of meaning — we want their future to be a meaningful one. So this is the central meeting-place of personal and impersonal values.

SELF-TRANSCENDENCE AND IDENTITY OVER TIME

I already cited Partridge on values that are outside the selves: people identify with, and seek to further, the well-being, preservation and endurance of communities, locations, causes, artifacts, institutions, ideals and so on, that they hope will flourish beyond their lifetimes.

I introduce the topic of self-transcendence by saying something about personal attachments and the related concept of love. Partridge does'nt mention persons. Still, personal attachments would seem to provide the most common instance of stepping outside oneself. But in his discussion of the corresponding concept of self-transcendence, Avner de-Shalit expresses some reservations about the relevance of personal attachments to our subject. He is critical of John Passmore's conception of a chain of love extending across time[198].

First, de-Shalit objects to the chain concept itself. Should we care for the children of our grand-children just because the latter care for them? De-Shalit does'nt see why; "love is not contagious". That may be true in general; but I wonder whether most people would'nt feel pangs of conscience when accused of indifference to the fate of their grand-children's offspring. I don't know how the importance of that motive could be calculated, but I think a discussion like ours should give it pride of place. Although I already remarked on its limitations, it does seem to generate an interest in the future that travels further than the medium range of current politics (so we get here an intriguing perspective on the complexities of social psychology). What should be noted however is that the motive does'nt stand alone: as I observed already, wishing our (great)-grand-children well carries the implication of wanting them to

---

[198] de-Shalit 1995, 32-33, 34f.

grow up in a society that offers meaningful options. So personal attachments let us share many other forward-looking values as well.

A further objection which de-Shalit formulates against the chain of love theory is that it is wrong to base obligations on sentiments (as Passmore seems to do), especially so when the sentiment in question is such an exclusive one as love for another person. I agree with de-Shalit's general point, but I consider that the concept of love then remains fully relevant for an analysis of psychologically supportive motives. It is true, of course, that "love", conceived as it generally is as an exclusive sentiment between persons, rapidly looses relevance when one is contemplating relations with the more distant future. However, it is possible to claim a broader use for the concept.In another context than the chain of love, Passmore himself gives to "love" a more general meaning. Although such phrases sound pretentious in our present age of debunking, we expect a judge to love the law, that is to care about the outcome of his decisions (as distinct from enjoying his own ingenuity); we expect a scientist to love truth; a statesman to love his country etc. Such as Passmore defines it, the concept seems indispensable for indicating the objectivity of serious concern.

> "To "love" is to take delight in the continuing existence of an object, to find it beautiful, to rejoice in its qualities and structure, and... to help it to survive and develop." It "goes beyond the enjoyment of the activity directed towards an object."[199]

It is clear that the capacity of loving, in that more general sense of the term, lies at the root of taking interest in states of affairs beyond one's own lifetime. What is at issue here is the defense of certain common sense truths against the assaults of contemporary subjectivism. How could one doubt with any measure of plausibility that if one wants something to happen, one indeed wants it to *happen* (during one's lifetime or later), instead of merely wanting to have the satisfaction of *believing* that it happens?[200]

I discussed love and objectivity; the next question is how the self constitutes itself by an investment in future good.

Avner-Shalit links self-transcendence with the unity of the self across time (he refers to Mac Intyre's narrative conception of the self). The self relates itself to its own past and future; for instance, it anticipates future experiences by hoping for the fulfilment of its present intentions.

---

[199]Passmore 1970, 299.

[200] de-Shalit 1995, 35 (cit.Brian Barry).

"There is no present which is not informed by some image of some future..."[201].

This is no mere psychology, it has a profoundly moral side to it. Moral deliberation is deliberation of agents who care about the integrity and meaningfulness of their actions over time, because they care about who they are as they travel through time. Our lives take shape only in time. Now, as de-Shalit formulates it, this continuity is not doomed to cease when one dies. Why should future events not count as implementations of present intentions? Philosophers usually talk about rational plans of life, in such a manner as to suggest that in striving to fulfill our ends, we cannot attach importance to states of affairs occurring after our own death. This suggestion is wrong in many instances. If I identify with some cause but won't see it win in my lifetime, it still matters to me whether I am under an illusion in wishing its success, or whether it really will gain a victory, although I won't be there to hear about it[202]. In other words, the concept of "identifying with" leads us beyond mere subjective feelings (it is not enough that I believe in my cause); in anticipating the fate of my acts and ideas after my death (in counting upon their positive contribution to the fund of knowledge, to world peace etc.), I constitute a part of my identity; and I submit that part of myself to the judgment of posterity. As de-Shalit formulates it, a part of one's identity during one's life is the expectation of the fate of one's acts and ideas after one's death. For instance, in putting forward some new scientific theory, I count on its being a fruitful one that will lead to further developments; that is, I actively anticipate its fruitfulness; I do not merely seek the satisfaction of believing in its worth, actual developments beyond my lifetime holding no interest for me. One does'nt want to pursue illusions. Nor do politicians, to take another example. Lenin has proved to be a failure in terms of his own expectations by recent events. As O'Neill sees it, the proper end from which an evaluation is to be made of somebody's life-story (whether it belongs to the tragic, comic or heroic genre) may occur a century or more after the person died[203]. It is important to notice that this is not just a question of posthumous reputation. The question of reputation is one of whether or not an achievement is recognized (it may be recognized for reasons that will prove to be wrong); the real issue is whether or not a work is an achievement, that is, whether it

---

[201] MacIntyre 1984, 215.

[202] de-Shalit 1995, 37-40, and O'Neill 1993, 31.

[203] O'Neill 1993, 31.

deserves recognition, and that, indeed, may be something which only future generations will be in a position to decide. So future generations can benefit or harm us:

> "the success or failure of our lives depends on them for it is they that are able to bring to fruition our projects"[204].

Whether they will actually do so depends, itself, upon their good will, or (more importantly perhaps) upon the inner worth of the project pursued, as it manifests itself over time. But this is accompanied, on the part of the living, by the expectation that future generations shall judge that inner worth according to certain conditions of rationality. We perhaps cannot miss the concept of sharing, with the future, a community of reasons. There is no sense in expecting the validity of Einstein's theories to be tested further by generations that have returned to Babylonian astrology.

One could say that self-transcendence takes many forms, shapes many undertakings and ways of life, that consequently make no sense unless they are able to reckon on a future that extends beyond our individual life-span. Science cannot be understood otherwise than as an enterprise that claims to have an indefinite future. Lawyers work for institutional continuities that keep society going on from one generation to the other. International politics are assessed by their contribution to the long-term aim of a peaceful and lawful world order.

There are many ways in which life finds a meaning by transcending its individual limits. But it should be remarked that meaningfulness does'nt depend on making a remarkable contribution to common enterprises oneself. The feeling of having done's one part, of having helped to keep the ship on course, is quite sufficient for most of us. Science, the arts, social life in general would'nt go on as they do without a great many forms of involvement of a largely anonymous kind. At its most simple and fundamental level, self-transcendence already shows in the desire to have children; one tacitly feels a part of the "great chain of being"[205].

---

[204] Ibid., 34.

[205] I am indebted to van Asperen 1993, 182. Cf.also ibid. 172-173 on the moral concept of "meaning". Van Asperen identifies life having a meaning with its being inserted in a wider framework, and criticizes the contemporary tendency to look upon that dimension of life as a merely private matter — which it in fact cannot be. Cf.also Taylor 1989, 97 on making sense of our lives by relating our own story to the greater pattern of realizing a good.

COMMUNITY

It is not difficult to perceive that communitarian forms of thought are more helpful for gaining insight in self-transcendence than individualist conceptions centred on personal choice. One has to be able to conceive of persons as forming their identity through an investment in projects, causes, pursuits that are recognized as valuable options within a certain society. Even before the concept of self-transcendence directs our attention towards the inter-generational aspects of meaning, it lets us perceive the basic truth that shared frameworks play a constitutive role in the actual workings of personal autonomy. It should be noticed in that connection that Passmore typically refers to shared meanings in order to instantiate the general sense of "love": he speaks of justice, beauty, the extension of knowledge etc.

Now one might raise the question whether self-transcendence in its relation to the future must be understood in a manner that draws still more heavily on a communitarian inspiration. Does it take the form of seeing the meanings we project into the future embodied in a particular social whole such as one's country? So that it is in the welfare of the future members of such a particular, all-purpose community that we are interested, in order to safeguard the values they shall presumably be sharing with us?

It is indeed difficult for the situated point of view, which is also the point of view of life and commitment, to imagine the transience of social wholes such as the country one lives in. Can we contemplate from the inside, as the respective nationals of these countries, the end of England, France, Holland, the US etc.? That would be identical with imagining the disappearance of what constitutes, for an important part, our transpersonal identity — a second death as it were. From the detached position, the position of the historian, human affairs offer no guarantee of continuity. Whole empires have sunk into oblivion. But that is not the position we take in daily life. We implicitly carry forward in our minds, into indefinite periods of time, such entities as the nations we are a citizen of. Future generations in a sense participate in that citizenship.

But it would be wrong to equate too quickly the idea of community with some closed, well-defined entity. Shared frameworks do not presuppose the existence of one single constituency. For instance, a scientist from Holland may have more to share with a colleague in China than with his countryman living next door.

Avner de-Shalit proposes the concept of the "transgenerational community"; that community, he says, is the moral and institutional reflection of the psychological idea of self-transcendence. I must refer the reader to his extensive treatment of the subject[206]. But let me summarize some main points. Avner de-Shalit first claims that behavioural indications abound of people identifying themselves with transgenerational communities of values, norms and ideas; for instance, we see ourselves as participating in some religious or political tradition, as exercising a craft or profession with a particular history, as being members of a national community etc., all of these extending over many generations. We understand the transgenerational community and all its members, no matter when they exist, as integral to ourselves and to what constitutes our identities. It is clear that these affiliations may overlap. According to de-Shalit, the existence of a transgenerational community depends on certain social conditions such as cultural interaction and moral similarity. The concept of "interaction" may cause surprise (I personally think "tradition" is the better choice); the essence of de-Shalit's position is to be found in the notion of an ongoing cultural, moral, and political debate about what the community stands for. That same idea is captured by MacIntyre's definition of tradition:

> "(living) tradition ... is an historically extended, socially embodied argument, and an argument precisely in part about the goods which constitute that tradition."[207]

Insofar as persons are individuated by their membership of traditions, the history of their lives is embedded in the larger narrative of such an argument about the good life.

Avner de-Shalit makes a rather forced (and, to my mind, unnecessary) attempt to use categories such as "interaction", "communication" or "dialogue" for the description of our relations with future generations. I think the use of such categories obscures the crucial difference between interaction and tradition. Temporal distance creates a fundamental divide between the two; it causes the ongoing "argument" of tradition to have a quite distinct structure, which makes one doubt whether it can be termed an argument at all. In an essay on the possibility of understanding history, Hans Jonas gives special emphasis to the point that present understanding has the aid of speech and counterspeech, whereas historical understanding has only the one-sided speech of the past.

---

[206] de-Shalit 1995, 13-50.

[207] MacIntyre 1981, 222. Cited by de-Shalit on p.44.

"As the past cannot come to the aid of our interpretation, neither can it defend itself against it." Historical communication is absolutely "monological".This does'nt mean that our interpretations must be arbitrary."Precisely because it is delivered into our hands, the residual speech of the past is entrusted to our most faithful care"[208].

We exercise such care against the background of confidence in a shared sameness of human beings — a confidence which is more heavily drawn upon where the originator and the recipient of the message cannot check with one another. But where something exists which we experience as a tradition, there also is a common focus: a certain unity of meaning is projected backwards and forwards in time. The history of a community shows the same pattern. I said that the life of an individual takes shape only in time. This is equally true of communities. If we are to deliberate and act purposively and responsibly in time, we must be able to see our common actions as fitting into meaningful patterns and practices through time[209]. Memory is the "bone and sinew" of our practical life, but so is hope and the search for common aims.

So much for a short excursion into communitarian theory, that has the sole ambition of showing its capacity for making us aware of intergenerational frameworks. Let me add the following observation. One might perhaps consider it to be somewhat inconsistent to seek support from communitarian insights and motives for a conception of justice between generations that finds its inspiration in Rawls' theory. That point finds an (at least partial) answer in the latter theory itself. Rawls wants to correct the impression that his whole theory is committed to purely individualistic values:

"(the) question remains whether the contract doctrine is a satisfactory framework for understanding the values of community"[210].

For instance, he warns us not to conceive the circumstances of justice as the description of an actual kind of social order (called by him "private society") where no one takes account of the good of others (i.e. where "each person assesses social arrangements solely as a means to his private aims"). The conditions incorporated in the original position stress the conflict of interests between persons in order to make the theory of justice depend on the

---

[208] Jonas 1974, 249-250.

[209] Gerald J.Postema, On the moral presence of our past (unpubl.paper).

[210] Rawls 1972, 520-521; see also 264-265. Cf.Mulhall & Swift 1996 for a detailed discussion.

weakest assumptions (some analogy may be found with Kant's dictum that one must be able to prove the advantage of social cooperation to a collection of devils); they do not pretend to describe a state of affairs that is acceptable from the point of view of human sociability.

That wider point of view finds an expression in Rawls' normative conception of reciprocity as a valued mode of living together (see 5.1.2) and in his idea of social union, which he extends to relations between generations and which I shall shortly mention under the heading of progress.

INTERGENERATIONAL COOPERATION

I argued that concern with the welfare of future generations first raises an issue for our understanding of the self. Now it is remarkable that in understanding the self through the concepts of self-transcendence and community, one is directly led beyond the self, in such a way as to transcend, with the self, its particular position in time. There is an identification with persons, places, projects, values, which causes us to take the longer view and which implies some sort of cooperation on the intergenerational level: there would be no sense in caring for those many goods that carry us, in our minds, beyond our own life-time, if we did expect those goods to be rejected by our descendants. On the contrary, it is constitutive of many concerns that future people are to benefit from them or that they are likely to pursue them[211]. We anticipate a confirmation of our understanding of the good, and a continuation of the efforts needed to realize it. For instance, large libraries or monuments are not built in order to be torn down the next day.

But the concept of intergenerational cooperation finds its most striking instance when we see people engaging in *projects* which would lose their point if future people could not be expected to continue them. Take for example the huge and continuous investments in research into nuclear fusion. That research depends on the cooperation of researchers of several generations; and according to recent forecasts, practical results may have to wait until the middle of next century. Another instance is provided by the policy of conserving biological resources: it will mainly benefit remote future people but impose burdens on present generations.

---

[211] Meyer 1997, 142. Meyer mentions the planting of trees that will not bear fruit for many years to come, land reclamation projects, investments in the conservation of knowledge and culture, the construction of large public monuments etc.

"Without their successor generations adopting a policy of the same kind and imposing certain burdens on themselves, present generations cannot achieve their goal of preserving these resources for remote future people. The goal of our policy, then, can be realized only if future generations are equally willing to bear the costs of the policy for the sake of remote future people. Only if there is intergenerational cooperation in achieving the goal of the policy, can the goal of the policy be realized." [212]

I related intergenerational cooperation to the achievement of value on the intergenerational level: one might say that the objective (impersonal) character of realizing value takes over (cf.also 4.4.1, note on objectivity). It then is a plain matter of consistency that we should allow future people to have the same chances of furthering value as we have. Your concern with the welfare of your (great-)grandchild involves a concern for *his* chances of working for the realization of aims that call for a vaster temporal horizon.

Now it might be objected, very plausibly, that the concept of intergenerational cooperation immediately evokes the contrary notion of future generations having the moral right *not* to confirm our values and *not* to pursue their realization. The objection would point out that in anticipating the cooperation of future people, we always start from our own, situated position within history, and that the "objectifying impulse" (Nagel), which lets us consider history from a more detached point of view, confronts us with an inevitable prospect of historical change. But this does'nt yet adress the moral side of the question. According to the present argument it is justice itself, the prime instance of a detached position, that calls for a recognition of every generation's moral right to define its particular conceptions of the good. I argue for this as follows. Justice between generations in respect of the environment was related to to the idea of equal liberty (through the concept of primary goods). It is clear that the latter idea must be interpreted in the (Rawlsian) sense in which it was introduced to start with. The term "generations" only serves as the indefinite indicator of persons occupying similar temporal position; persons share the competence to pursue their own conception of the good; more precisely, Rawls defines persons (within the realm of the political) as individuals capable of reflecting upon and revising the attachments they happen to have, the goods they happen to be committed to. The liberal insistence on the faculty of critical revision finds an evident context in the relations between generations, when these relations are

---

[212] Ibid., 143.

conceived in terms of an "historically extended argument" about the good (MacIntyre).

So the detached position, with its emphasis on equal liberty, must affect our anticipations with a fundamental doubt. We say to future generations: this is what we want to do for you, or what we want you to carry on for the benefit of people still more remote in time. But we say also: of course, you have the fullest right to say no. The question is, how these two sorts of (tacit) affirmations can be put forward at the same time. At first sight, the answer just lies in ourselves, the living, taking a modest position: let us work for the future according to our own lights, but with a healthy sense of our historical limitations. That answer, I think, is too easy. The background reality is one of conflict — conflict between the situated and the detached view. I think there is no way in which we can internalize, make ours, the full potential scale of historical change, such as we become conscious of when we occupy the detached position. Moreover, it is no mere question of persons individually facing one another across time. The conceptions which the detached position wants us to leave, in its abstract way, to the discretion of posterity, are the conceptions we always share (at least in the form of some consensus concerning acceptable options) within the framework of a certain society, of a certain culture, or of humanity at large at a certain moment of history.

In choosing the detached perspective, we concede the right of critical revision to our descendants, but we do so with tacit reservations. Are we for instance prepared to contemplate, as a concrete possibility, the wholesale rejection of that same liberal philosophy which underwrites our concession in the first place? Let us note also that the concept of critical revision presupposes certain conditions of rationality. Would we consider it for example to be a critical revision of reigning values if a liberal society were overrun by a fundamentalist theocracy?

I emphasized the factor of discontinuity — cooperation being hoped for from future generations, on the basis of present commitments and beliefs, but being threatened at the same time by important changes in shared conceptions of the good. That factor of discontinuity has a strong impact on the following issue: whether it is possible to assert that we owe a duty of respect to our predecessor's sacrifices and savings (sacrifices and savings possibly intended to benefit not only us but more remote people as well) that would be based itself on a duty of respect owed to the valuable activities of other people in general, and that would enjoin us (the living) not to dispose of, or use up what has been created by these activities?[213]

I shall go along (cf.5.2.2) with Joseph Raz' general position that everyone has a duty of respect towards the values which give meaning to human life, even to those on which one's own life does not depend for its meaning. For instance, even if I am no lover of art, I have no moral right to destroy a painting by van Gogh that is in my possession. But transferring that precept to intergenerational relations is no easy matter. The van Gogh example already shows that some common understanding of value is being presupposed: I am no lover of art, but I know that there is a general consensus about the status of van Gogh as a great artist. So the question is, in what measure (if any) this sort of argument can be made to work on the intergenerational level.

We must set aside, as belonging to another sort of consideration, the duty of fairness discussed in section 4.2 above. Take generations A,B and C. It can be argued that if generation A, in saving resources for generation B, has intended to start an intergenerational practice of savings that would not have existed otherwise (or not on a similar scale), and if generation B accepts to benefit from these savings, there is a case for holding that generation B has a duty of fairness to continue the practice in favour of generation C. But this is not, or not precisely, the moral issue I want to adress. Generation B's duty of fairness is based on the circumstance that it accepts to profit from the practice, and so must be loyal to it. The question, what generation A may have been right to anticipate as being of benefit to generation B then is beside the point. On the contrary, the moral issue I referred to above was, whether a norm of respect for activities on account of their *value* can be relied upon in order to ground an intergenerational duty of transmission (where the transmitting generation does'nt necessarily have to be a beneficiary itself!).

The crux of the matter is that we cannot really expect a generation to have a duty of respect towards ideas, objects, institutions or whatever which it is'nt prepared to consider itself as having some positive value. We presently judge it to be self-evident that the Parthenon or the Sistine chapel be conserved for posterity, but we don't think we have to trouble about the sentimental *genre* paintings popular in the Paris salons of the 1850's (I hear that most of them have disappeared, even from museum cellars). The 1850 public had a high appreciation of these paintings and gave them pride of place in its museums (presumably, in order to benefit future generations as well)!

---

[213] Cf.Meyer 1997, 148.

So it seems that the sacrifices and savings of former generations can only justify a duty of transmission within the outer limits of ourselves, the living, ratifying the value of those sacrifices and savings, on the basis of a creative intercourse with tradition. O'Neill claims that

> "our primary responsibility is to attempt, as far as it is possible, to ensure that future generations do belong to a community with ourselves — that they are capable, for example, of appreciating works of science and art, the goods of the non-human environment.."etc.[214].

I agree. But when he adds that

> "(This) is an obligation not only to future generations, but also to those of the past, so that their achievements continue to be both appreciated and extended"[215],

I take it that he tacitly agrees with the reservation I just argued for. A duty of respect owed to the valuable activities of our ancestors can have no more solid basis than is provided for it by the ongoing determination of value itself. So we cannot ourselves *demand* respect for our values from future generations. On the other hand (and here we have the conflict again), no values exist without commitment, and so we would be inconsistent with ourselves if we tried to anticipate (in what way?) their being subjected to future change. Our values themselves oblige us to *hope* for their being confirmed and developed by future people. O'Neill is right to stress the responsibility we have in regard to them, and our capacity to do something about it.

All the same, one should recognize that a duty of respect towards past achievements and intentions appears to be beyond dispute in many cases. Meyer gives the example of an advanced system of tertiary education inherited from our predecessors, and presumably built up in order to benefit remote future people as well. It would be wrong for us to neglect the investments, the personnel policies etc. that are needed to its being maintained over time, for the sake of achieving higher levels of welfare in the present[216]. Future people could blame us for not having respected our predecessor's sacrifices and good intentions in bequeathing public goods to both us and them. It is not, in this

---

[214] O'Neill 1993, 34.

[215] Ibid.: "...and to the present.. so that we do not ...undermine our own achievements by rendering impossible our own success."

[216] Meyer 1997, 148.

example, that we would refuse to recognize the value of tertiary education as such; it rather is that we would have preferred other goods to that system of education being continued across time, and that this choice would be wrong because of its lack of respect for the intentions that caused us to inherit the system of education in the first place (a system to which we confer value ourselves).

But the broad tenor of this section has been that the intergenerational dimension of value creates a moral space characterized by the tension between the detached and the situated view. It is perhaps inherent in our condition of historical beings that there is no general solution to it.

This should inspire some healthy suspicion in regard to the use of apparently harmonizing concepts like "debate" or "argument" for characterizing relations between generations.

TIMELESS VALUE

It is certainly no characteristic of contemporary thought to make room for pretensions of eternal validity (the rules of logics, mathematical truth, or the basic physical constituents of the universe being excepted?). The general intellectual atmosphere is better symbolized by those works of art ("self-destructs") whose "art" function leaves no trace because it consists in the melting process of a wax structure. But one wonders whether such an exaltation of the evanescent has deep roots. Take the people queuing for a great exhibition of classical painting: their perception of a Vermeer, a Rembrandt, is of an exactly opposite sort. These works of art ("classic" works) are felt to have an existence of its own, a necessary one that places them beyond the sphere of the contingent. Once we have seen them, we cannot imagine them not to exist (it is indeed difficult to accept that they have'nt existed before they were created). We do not perceive them as objects to which we *confer* value, a value depending on subjective choice; we perceive them as *having* it, in a necessary and thus timeless manner.

I do not want to enter into the ontological aspects of such an experience. I only want to suggest that it carries an implicit claim: the claim to an open future, an eternal one in fact. We cannot enjoy Vermeer's "View of Delft" and not consider as absurd the eventuality of its destruction (or even of its losing a public). So we have a strong motive for securing the material and social conditions of its conservation. Its destruction (or for that matter a complete change in aesthetic values) can of course be quietly envisaged by the detached point of view. But we have here again an instance of the tragic and unavoidable clash between the two perspectives on the world. We perhaps can envisage the destruction of Vermeer's "View of Delft", but can we live with such a prospect?

I mentioned contemporary instances of an exaltation of the evanescent. In a provocative essay on modernity, George Steiner claims that an ideology of the "happening" and of autodestructive artifacts "with their emphasis on the immediacy, unrepeatability, and ephemeral medium of the work" is contrary to the very concept of culture[217]. The following passage is wholly relevant to our subject.

> "The thrust of will which engenders art and disinterested thought, the engaged response which alone can ensure its transmission to other human beings, to the future, are rooted in a gamble on transcendence. The writer or thinker means the words of the poem, the sinews of the argument, the personae of the drama, to outlast his own life, to take on the mystery of autonomous presence and greatness. The sculptor commits to the stone the vitalities against and across time which will soon drain from his own living hand. Art and mind adress those who are not yet, even at the risk, deliberately incurred, of being unnoticed by the living."[218] Whatever production of the spirit we contemplate, "(each) time, the equation is one of ambitious sacrifice, of the obsession to outlast, to outmaneuver the banal democracy of death."[219]

So it is curious to find Hans Jonas making peace with the "undeniable fact" that the modern temper is uncongenial to the idea of immortality[220]. I wonder whether the admittedly ironical way in which we presently tend to consider any explicit pretension to immortality warrants a conclusion contrary to Steiner's perception of culture as a gamble on transcendence (at least in its higher forms). As Jürgen Moltmann formulates it in his "Theology of Hope,"

> "An acceptance of the present which cannot and will not see the dying of the present is an illusion and a frivolity."[221]

I myself don't see how a concrete notion of solidarity with future generations can be entertained unless we keep open the door for the ambition

---

[217] Steiner 1971, 92-93.

[218] Ibid., 89.

[219] Ibid., 90.

[220] Jonas 1996, 115f. However, Jonas develops a metaphysics of "eternity" manifesting itself in the moment of existential decision.

[221] Moltmann 1967, 32.

to transcend by acts of creation or commitment our own empirical life-form, and unless we presume or at least hope for the ongoing validity of what we presently consider to be our cultural heritage. There must be some confidence in values to be shared. The practice of spending money for the construction of vast national libraries and museums, the Unesco program for the conservation of the great monuments of mankind etc., would have no sense without such confidence being had as a matter of course. We all feel that future generations have a moral right to the enjoyment of our cultural treasures.

I cited Steiner on culture and transcendence;

> "the very core of the concept of culture will have been broken ... (if) the gamble on transcendence no longer seems worth the odds and we are moving into a utopia of the immediate"[222]

and I doubted whether our ironical modes of discourse (and art) reflect the basic reality of contemporary culture (except the self-destructive artifacts, of course).

However, the other side of the medal is that we do live in a highly ambiguous cultural context, since the assumption of an ongoing validity, which we cannot do without as concerns central instances of culture, still has to compete in our minds with a very general and influential conception of the inevitability of historical change. There is a sharp awareness of the transient character of our ways of life and cultural patterns. Take the example of painting: whatever confidence we may have in our present standards of taste, we know that rather different standards ruled the judgment of museum directors some 100 years ago, and so we expect that judgment to be different again within the next 100 years. That expectation is an abstract one, it is true. We expect change, but we don't know in what direction; no concrete images compete with the present models of taste; all the same, confidence in present standards is undermined.

PROGRESS

I just said that confidence in contemporary values is undermined by our pervasive consciousness of historical change, with a consequent loss of nourishment for feelings of solidarity with future generations. Now this assertion needs to be qualified in a very serious way, as our consciousness of historical change originates, itself, in a sense of progress that has run parallel to certain material and mental developments in Western society

---

[222] Steiner 1971, 93.

since the Middle Ages. The notion that human affairs show lines of progress towards the future, that time itself is directional in terms of certain important goods, makes the feeling of change a very different thing from the mere awareness of continuous but unpredictable evolution. I think the latter form of consciousness rather characterizes our present situation at the end of the century: insofar, the sense of change remains with us after having lost contact with its historical roots.

Conceptions of historical progress form a powerful motive for securing the future chances of society and culture. Our individual life gets a transpersonal significance; it derives its meaning from participation in a greater pattern that does'nt suffer (on the contrary) from reaching beyond the horizon of our own lives. Self-transcendent meaning finds a direction in the shared story we can tell.

It is interesting to note that Rawls' argument on future generations develops within the framework of a time-related understanding of society. The issue of justice between generations as it is pictured by his theory is raised by the vision of society as a system of cooperation between generations over time. We meet future generations in our minds as partners in a historical undertaking; so they partly lose their anonymity. Another perspective on the temporal dimension of society (also very much related to the idea of progress) is offered by Rawls' concept of "social union"[223]. As Rawls puts it himself, the question arises whether the principles of justice and their justification (the "contract doctrine") provide a satisfactory framework for understanding the good of community; the "congruence of the right and the good" depends in large part upon whether a well-ordered society realizes the values that inhere in human sociability; now in defining the latter, Rawls emphasizes that

> "it is through social union founded upon the needs and potentialities of its members that each person can participate in the total sum of the realized natural assets of the others". It is "a basic characteristic of human beings that no one person can do everything that he might do"; so "different persons with similar or complementary capacities may cooperate so to speak in realizing their common or matching nature". "We are led to the notion of the community of mankind the members of which enjoy one another's excellences and individuality elicited by free institutions"[224]

---

[223] Rawls 1971, 523-524.
[224] Rawls 1971, 523

Rawls suggests that this community may also be imagined to extend over time. He refers to Kant's "Idea for a universal history". Every individual man would have to live for a vast length of time if he were to learn how to make complete use of all his natural capacities, and therefore it will require perhaps an incalculable series of generations of men.

Now it is impossible to ignore that such directional conceptions of history carry a threat to the very notion of equality that is at the basis of our intuition of intergenerational justice. If historical development is conceived as being, fundamentally, directed by a central *telos* (by progress towards a desired end state), no lack of precedents exist for letting such a conception rule over the whole field of value, and impose heavy sacrifices affecting the worth of liberty on the generations that don't have the luck of being at the receiving end. Those intermediate generations should be happy enough to participate in the construction of Paradise.

No wonder that Rawls rejects any such totalitarian conception of the good, which leaves no room for the independent force of considerations of justice, and more generally runs counter to his pluralistic convictions. No intergenerationally distributive setting (in Rawls' case: savings) allows particular generations to derive stronger claims than others from their mere position in time. Justice between generations makes it impossible to consider the desired end state of society "as that alone which gives meaning and purpose to the whole process"[225]. All generations have their appropriate aims. Rawls apparently considers the threat to intergenerational disequilibrium to take an utilitarian form: he rejects, in the name of intergenerational equality, the notion of an intergenerational calculus of advantages balancing the losses of some against the benefits of others. But one wonders whether the surplus value of Utopia depends for its defenders upon such a rational calculus at all.

The criticism of totalitarian conceptions of progress leaves us with the problem, how to consider the relation between individual ends and the shared values whose realization is presumed to govern historical change. No sacrificial implication exists if one considers every generation to do its part in realizing the desired end state (a generational participation that lets individual self-transcendence find a shared expression), while every generation at the same time derives an advantage from the whole process by standing at a higher plane of welfare or culture than the preceding one. In principle, at least, such a gradual approach seems to answer the natural objection against people

---

[225] Rawls 1971, 289.

being supposed to sacrifice major interests to the coming of "better days they won't see themselves", simply because they happen to occupy an intermediate position in the great march of history. Of course, this leaves individuals free to sacrifice everything to such a better future: what is at stake here — once a premise of justice between generations has been firmly put into place! — is solely the exclusion of mere position in time as a reason that would justify the sacrifice of equal liberty.

Naturally, modest conceptions of progress that do not pretend to govern the whole field of value (such as Kant's concept of world peace) don't generate this problem at all.

But is the issue of sacrificial progress, with its direct threat to intergenerational justice, a serious one within the environmental context? I doubt it, since sacrifices in environmental quality (e.g. acceptance of widespread industrial pollution in order to facilitate rapid industrial growth, in the former Soviet fashion) may often turn out to involve irreversible damage. So what future Paradise would one have been working for?

Now it is a striking fact that our 20th century experience with Utopia makes us presently avoid any explicit discourse on large historical aims, whether those aims are of the utopian sort or not. Does that herald "the end of history", or is it a transitory phenomenon? It is interesting to listen to Steiner again: as a gamble on transcendence, culture is joined to a gamble on progress, which opens the dimension of the future as it were. The following passage concludes his argument on progress, which covers many aspects of recent history and to which I gladly refer.

> "The whole issue of a working theory of culture in the absence of a dogma or genuinely felt metaphoric imperative of progress and perfectibility seems to me one of the most difficult now facing us. The key diagnostic insight is that of Dante when he analyzes the exact condition of prophecy in Hell: ...("You may understand, therefore/ That all our knowledge shall be a dead thing from the moment on/ When the door of the future is shut.")... "Close the door of the future" — that is, relinquish the ontological axiom of historical progress — and "all knowledge" is made inert."[226]

But the question perhaps is whether the (transitory?) absence of an imperative of progress and perfectibility, while characterizing according to Steiner the higher levels of culture, reflects the "inner truth" of other less articulate sectors of social reality. When one considers the personal investment

---

[226] Steiner 1971, 73. The citation from Dante is from Inferno, 10.

of many people in such enterprises as the development of science, the search for peace, the struggle for human rights etc., or for that matter the joyful reception given to new forms of communication such as the Internet, one wonders whether that imperative, though not shared at present on the level of our accepted modes of discourse, does'nt stay very much alive on the level of day-to-day reality.

I want to distinguish, from the notion of progress proper, the circumstance that the aim of securing a sustainable economy subjects society as a whole to constraints that put a premium on having a public debate about our common purposes. It is becoming clear that the search for effective environmental policies must result in a critical attitude towards our entire way of life (as it is based for instance on the automobile): an attitude which considers contemporary society from the angle of the value presuppositions it shares rather than from a pluralist perspective that is too often taken for granted.

CRITICAL REFLECTIONS ON CONTEMPORARY CULTURE

I already suggested the importance for our subject of a critical reflection on contemporary culture in my discussion of the topics of timeless value and of progress. I now wish to mention two aspects of modern life which seem to be of the greatest interest for any attempt to elucidate its attitude towards the long-term future. Philosophy must here adress the relation between patterns of thought and an omnipresent social reality.

In his recent book on ecology and politics, John O'Neill makes an interesting attempt to relate contemporary thought structures to general traits of the society we live in. His starting-point is a manifestly perfectionist view on human well-being, the desirable capacities and attributes of persons being derived by him, in an Aristotelian vein, from certain ideals or conceptions of the person[227]. He rejects a conception of the good in terms of subjective states of mind (want satisfaction), which leaves no room for reasoned argument. This permits him to defend environmental values on qualitative grounds, which in his view may overrule our common but fallible perceptions of the good. For instance, the consumer has a narrower conception of the good life than the citizen (both roles being often combined by the same person!): there is what I *want* and there is what we *value*. Now, O'Neill stresses that our

---

[227] O'Neill 1993, 180: ..."the development of human capacities within the sciences and arts, ... opens humans to the goods around them ... (and) also place individuals within an historical tradition in which the well-being of those in the present is tied to that of those in the future...".

perceptions of the good find an embodiment in particular social contexts and institutions. He claims that the narrow, subjectivist account of human well-being very much reflects the dominating position of the market economy, which fosters mobility and undermines all traditions. A "temporal myopia" infects modern society;

> "our projects, and interests in the success of such projects, are not understood as tied to the future"[228].

So the problem of obligations to future generations "is a social and political problem concerning the economic, social and cultural conditions for the existence and expression of identity that extends across generations"[229].

According to O'Neill, what we need is to develop forms of community which place individuals within the framework of a common tradition. An ecologically rational society requires an institutional context in which interests are not defined in the sole terms of an unlimited acquisition of material goods[230].

This relates the whole issue of time and value — of our orientation on the future — to a fundamental criticism of modernity. The dominance of economic man is in fact described in such all-encompassing terms that one wonders what resources are left for the critical attitude itself. Are we held captive by some massive, self-imposed determinism? And if mobility and the disappearance of all traditions form a basic configuration of modern times, what room is left for intergenerational values such as the commitment to a certain way of life or to the perpetuation of a certain community? O'Neill's description of modernity echoes Marx' picture of capitalism in the Communist Manifesto:

> "Constant revolutionizing of production, uninterrupted disturbance of all social conditions, everlasting uncertainty and agitation distinguish the bourgeois epoch from all earlier ones. All fixed, fast-frozen relations, with their train of ancient and venerable prejudices and opinions are swept away, all new-

---

[228] Ibid., 38.
[229] Ibid., 42.
[230] Ibid., 180.

formed ones become antiquated before they can ossify. All that is solid melts into air, all that is holy is profaned."[231]

What concrete ideas do we entertain with any confidence about the way of life of our descendants, even within the short time frame of the next hundred years? Science fiction stories fill a whole department in our bookshops, but what criteria do we have for judging their plausibility?

I just mentioned science fiction: it is perhaps the development of science and technology which creates the most manifest obstacle to filling out the future with images of what it is going to bring, and so makes that future even more abstract for us than it would be otherwise[232]. It does so while causing, at the same time, a constant rupture with tradition, which condemns the past to being an object of noncommittal curiosity. It has been said that we are progressively entering into a third age of social time (meaning: a third age of our collective conceptions of time) which is different from the mythical, cyclical time of traditional societies, and from the linear, directional time of the modern notion of progress: the radically uncertain, apparently "random" time of techno-science, which is freed from any connection with a meaning either borrowed from the past or projected into the future. So that future is clothed in obscurity. Modern science is creative, its inventions are unforeseeable (by definition), it is experimental by nature. Who could have foreseen the information society we are presently entering in? Our whole society has turned experimental. It is a paradox of our age that it is the same society which has made its own future an unforeseeable one, which must take responsibility for damage it is causing within an unprecedented time-scale. No images of future life seem to support it in adopting that moral point of view; we don't know what new worlds we are going to get. Because of its unforeseeable development, the same mastery over nature which extends our collective responsibility over a much larger time horizon robs us of a picture of future society that could help to bring future generations closer to us in our minds.

Again, this sort of explanation of contemporary trends should find a place within a general inquiry into our collective (socially ratified) conceptions of

---

[231] Marx & Engels 1992, 6. It is interesting to compare this diagnosis of modernity with Alexis de Tocqueville's in Democracy in America II, 2, 2, where it is individualism and the general mobility of the status of persons which creates a constant break with the past and lets us have no idea of those who will follow us (".. .la trame des temps se rompt à tout moment, et le vestige des générations s'efface. On oublie aisément ceux qui vous ont précédé, et l'on n'a aucune idée de ceux qui vous suivront.")

[232] I feel indebted to van der Pot 1985, 176f, and to Ost 1985, 122.

time, such as they have evolved through history. These conceptions fashion, or at least influence, our basic attitudes in the field of time and value. Different conceptions may be at work at the same time. In fact, I wonder whether this is not very much the case in our confused present circumstances. Let me suggest that modern man has evolved, since the 18th century, a largely historicist turn of mind. He sees change all around him and so gets used to thinking in terms of change. Now what we witness at present is the coexistence of two conceptions of time as change: the directional one of wanted change ("progress"), and the more haphazard one of scientific and technological experiment. Needless to say that the directional element, the search for common blueprints for a better life, better anchors the sense of solidarity with future generations. But do we still experience history as ascendant at the end of this century?

5.2.2 Trust in the future as a primary good

My intention in the above paragraphs has been to suggest that a strong case can be made out for the cross-generational character of our experience of the good. Let me assume for a moment its unqualified validity. Care for long-term environmental needs secures a shared condition for pursuing worthwhile activities, namely the capacity to engage in these activities within an intergenerational framework of meaning. Environmental policies with long-term goals or implications provide for an essential condition of our experience of the good and thus of living a meaningful life, namely, trust in the perpetuation on this planet of conditions for a decent life. If we want to characterize this in a Rawlsian way, the concept of a primary good is a plausible candidate. Primary goods

> "are singled out by asking which things are generally necessary as social conditions and all-purpose means to enable persons to pursue their determinate conceptions of the good"[233].

In chapter 4, I said that environmental goods represent a category of primary goods that has the vocation of securing the fair value of liberty. I now want to claim that the full measure of such a fair value depends on confidence in an open future for human society, beyond our own expected span of life. So one can say that in caring for an equal claim of all generations on the resources of the planet (primary good in a first sense: capacity for having a minimum of options at all, beyond the level of a life that is "brutal, nasty and

---

[233] Rawls 1993, 307.

short), justice between generations also cares for equality in respect of an essential condition of *meaningful* life (primary good in a second sense: opportunity to serve values which claim a larger time frame than one's individual life).

Let us now admit some doubts about the general validity of the thesis that our experience of the good has a cross-generational dimension. Does collecting postage stamps or gardening have it? And what about an unsophisticated enjoyment of the present day? A philosophical argument with a "perfectionist" slant may find reasons for attributing to such goods a lesser quality. But in pursuing this line of thought, one encounters an interesting problem in political philosophy. For one lets long-term environmental protection serve a particular conception of the good, and does'nt that offend against the principle of neutrality? (I define "neutrality" in the usual sense of the state avoiding judgments about the relative merits of ends of life in the justification of its action.) The question in a way is an academic one, since we are dealing here with a justification of state action where the first line of argument consists in invoking shared physical needs. So what is at issue is whether the protection of the environmental interests of future generations (which raises no neutrality issue by itself) could be said to have unavoidably partisan *effects*.

The issue is a complex one. I discuss it by making the following points.

1. I note to start with that Rawls' theoretical framework could certainly accomodate, without compromising its political stand-off in respect of our many conceptions of the good, a justification of state intervention that would be based on the assumption that it is a general (overall) feature of our experience of the good to have a cross-generational dimension (an assumption I just questioned).

Rawls' theory raises no general obstacles against acknowledging the facts of our moral phenomenology. For instance, Rawls admits the validity of many claims made by his communitarian critics as regards the role of our value commitments in building our identity. What he denies is that this way of regarding ourselves is appropriate for the purpose of politics, because it would result in making our identity as citizens depend on whether or not we established or maintained a particular moral identity (for example, a particular belief)[234]. Our identity as citizens must remain the same whatever changes we may undergo in our personal commitments: this is what is captured by the

---

[234] Cf. for a clear exposition: Mulhall & Swift 1996.

original position, which stipulates that the parties do know that they have a conception of the good without knowing what it is. They are conceived as being independent from such conceptions and as being capable of revising them on reasonable grounds. But it would not be contrary to the spirit of that position if one were to inform the parties that our experiences and conceptions of the good have, intrinsically, an intergenerational character. In doing so, one would merely provide them with a knowledge of general facts; such knowledge is allowed by the stipulations of the original position. It would'nt result in making our identity as citizens depend on a particular category of moral commitments.

2. Now let me recall the doubts formulated at the beginning of this section. Is confidence in an indefinitely open future for human society indeed a general precondition for pursuing the ends of life that are commonly thought to be valuable? One's first impression is that a negative answer would cause some friction with the spirit of Rawls' theory. Confidence in the long-term future would be reduced to a requirement inherent in an important, but not all-inclusive category of possible ends of life. Insofar, a measure of *de facto* partisanship would indeed seem to be unavoidable in state action providing for the environmental long-term.

I think a first way of avoiding that conclusion would consist in arguing that it is irrelevant whether securing the physical conditions of future human life actually favours some particular and presently held conception of the good; what one should note is that it guarantees, on an overall front, the conditions of an ongoing argument about the good.

The conception of the person defended by Rawls as the right one within the political realm is one of individuals capable of reflecting upon and revising the attachments they happen to have, the goods they happen to be committed to. Now this liberal insistence on the faculty of critical revision finds an even more appropriate context in the relations between generations. Our individual capacities of reflection and revision are always exercised within the social framework of an ongoing debate about the good; within the most various areas, that debate moves from one generation to the other. For instance, chess players participate in a history of chess with its classics and its interest in developing newer strategies.

3. I just suggested that no neutrality issue complicates the recourse to a Rawlsian framework when one insists on the role of environmental protection in "keeping open the doors of history", i.e. in sustaining conditions for the exercise of the faculty of critical revision. Another possible line of argument

might consist in the claim that those forms of the good that commit us to the long-term view represent core elements of culture, and that a rich cultural background is essential for the value of liberty. Freedom should not be considered in the abstract, it depends on the range of options one is able to choose from. Could this argument justify the introduction of cultural values within Rawls' domain of the political[235]?

I cannot pretend to settle the issue within the framework of the present discussion. I merely wish to recall the headlines of an argument developed by Joseph Raz, which supports (in the name of the liberal value of autonomy) a non-partisan promotion of cultural pluralism, and which I consider to be relevant to our own topic[236]. That argument cannot be directly assimilated by Rawls' theory. Raz rejects Rawls' separation between "the right" and "the good", and puts forward a straightforwardly perfectionist view on the legitimate functions of government. Raz makes a sharp difference between liberalism considered as a political doctrine putting personal freedom at the centre, and individualism considered as a moral theory. A liberal does not have to be an individualist; he can very well believe that collective goods have a constitutive (i.e. more than instrumental) importance for personal autonomy. Freedom has no content unless its exercise is inspired by substantive values that shape the general character of society. All this could probably be accepted by Rawls, except for political purposes *stricto sensu*. But Raz reinforces his position by an explicit rejection of the principle of neutrality: government must stimulate the pursuit of worthwhile activities and discourage the pursuit of morally worthless ones (coercion being excluded of course, because it conflicts with the ideal of autonomy)[237].

For Raz, this does not involve a plea for partisan attitudes. Raz resists the individualist reading of social reality as a mere addition of individuals following separate lives inspired by separate conceptions of the good; when stimulating particular conceptions of the good, government can invoke, against the criticism that it is taking sides, the value of enriching society as the setting of liberty, by increasing the spectrum of social choice. It can say that it is

---

[235] I refer to Mulhall & Swift, op.cit.,p.226-227.

[236] Joseph Raz, The morality of freedom, Oxford 1986.

[237] Raz apparently thinks that what is *not* "worthwhile" can be identified by the state without serious qualms. I do not discuss this issue, the spectrum of what we all consider to be worthwhile (or at least consider to represent a respectable option) being wide enough.

increasing the worth of liberty. An additional ground for perfectionist state intervention is found by Raz (within the same anti-individualist perspective) in the circumstance that many options cannot be had at all unless they are embodied within certain general features of society (called by Raz collective goods[238]).

According to Raz,

"A person is autonomous only if he has a variety of acceptable options to choose from..."[239].

The variety concept is strengthened on the moral side by Raz' belief that the values we live by are shared in that weaker sense of the word that we may all of us live according to separate and incommensurable conceptions of the good, but that we have to regard our different goals and tastes

"as valuable because they exemplify universal values or values which form part of a mosaic which in its entirety makes for valuable social life"[240].

For instance, Raz affirms that destroying a van Gogh painting one owns is "to show oneself blind to one of the values which give life a meaning"; as owner of the painting, I have a duty to preserve it "regardless of whether I profess to be a lover of art". Raz adds that

"everyone has a duty of respect towards the values which give meaning to human life, even to those on which one's life does not depend for its meaning"[241].

---

[238] "Collective goods" are a sub-category of "public goods". A good is a public good if the distribution of its benefits is not subject to control by anyone other than each potential beneficiary, the degree to which the latter benefits depending on his character, interests, and dispositions.- As concerns environmental interests, it is clear that the relevant "collective good" if formed by what one might call the sustainable character of society i.e. the complex of structural features (political, legal, economic, cultural) that work against an irreversible loss of ecological resources. Such a "general beneficial feature of society" is a shared social resources whose benefits are diffuse (Raz himself mentions instances like society being a tolerant or educated one).

[239] Raz, op.cit.p.204.

[240] Ibid., 215. A somewhat similar conception underlies Rawls' concept of "social union", which he extends to relations over time.

[241] Ibid.p.212.

This is not only a question of respect for values; it also is a crucial issue for the development of normal personal relations that one recognize the value of other people's options, even though one does not pursue them oneself[242].

It follows from this line of argument that as they ensure the opportunity for pursuing many activities we all are bound to value as options that together make up the very core of our civilization and thus give a meaning to liberty, policies securing trust in a sufficient degree of ecological continuity should not be judged on apparently partisan implications. A political stand-off..."would undermine the chances of survival of many cherished aspects of our culture"[243].

Meyer offers an appropriate concept by developing the notion of "living in a society that is open to the future". For those many contemporaries who pursue future-oriented projects,

> "it is important for their well-being that they can place the pursuit of their projects in an ongoing and unfolding story. In particular it is important to them that they can expect the continuance of human life on earth under such conditions that future people will be able to understand the point and value of the projects they have been pursuing, that they can make good use of them or may choose to continue them. Being able meaningfully to choose a project whose success partly depends on intergenerational cooperation presupposes living in a society of a certain quality"[244].

Let us consider for instance scientific research or long-term investments in the sphere of education: society must care for the material conditions of future people's capacity to make good use of their results and to continue them. This certainly calls for future levels of welfare well above the level of survival. Meyer follows Raz' conception of society by claiming that living in a society that is open to the future is a valuable feature for all members of society, as its concern for the conditions of strongly future-oriented activities enriches the general spectrum of choice in an important way. The opportunity to live in a society that is open to the future can itself be understood as a public good in Raz' sense.

4. The question of partisan implications was generated by the observation that environmental policies might as a matter of fact further the realization of particular conceptions of the good (though raising no neutrality issue on a first

---

[242] Ibid.pp.215-216.

[243] Ibid.p.162.

[244] Meyer 1997, 143.

line of argument). But it is a remarkable feature of the contemporary situation that environmental aims may need to be made effective by policies which *purposely* discriminate between conceptions of the good, without the principle of neutrality being infringed all the same. Let me explain as follows.

There is a widely shared conviction that effective environmental policies demand a critical attitude towards our contemporary way of life. Now if environmental protection on a large scale requires an active pursuit of social change, it requires *ipso facto* that the state must discriminate between different conceptions of the valuable ends of life. For instance, the view is gaining ground that the warming of the planet can only be counteracted by measures that strongly limit the use of the automobile, favour more moderate uses of energy etc., some conceptions of the good being thereby supported, and others discouraged. From a wider ethical point of view, a strong case can be made for the proposition that the ecological crisis can only be overcome by the cultivation of virtues quite different from those which modernity has put a premium on.

So there is a chance that environmental policies shall depend for their effectiveness on the state taking sides in the social debate on conceptions of the good. However, the state will not be doing so on the basis of a perfectionist philosophy, but in order to implement an uncontroversial task of government. The situation can be described in terms of the contrast between a "neutrality of aim" (which anti-perfectionist liberals ask the government to respect) and a "neutrality of effect" (which cannot be guaranteed). As the principle of neutrality only refers to neutrality in the first-mentioned sense, no breach with it occurs in the present instance. What one discovers (in Rawlsian terms) is that a particular primary good (trust in a decent measure of social continuity) must be paid for by qualifying (for instrumental reasons) the liberal premise that a modern state can and should avoid passing judgment on conceptions of the good.

5.3 A PHILOSOPHICAL CHALLENGE

If we consider it to be the task of philosophy to clarify our moral reactions (while subjecting them to its own critical resources), it is clear that an explanation of the intuition that justice must be done to future generations, that tries to find the proper place for that intuition within a theory of justice and a supporting theory of value, belongs to the more ambitious part of its programme. It is a many-sided undertaking which the present argument has only been able to explore in a tentative way. I think any such exploration is bound to discover the philosophically very provocative nature of the subject, carrying us beyond all the frontiers we draw around some neat conception of "relevant" philosophy. If I had to answer the question, what central problem of philosophical method I consider to be raised by the topic of intergenerational concern, I would perhaps suggest that a discussion of the subject typically resists certain prevalent frames of thought because the latter combine to rob it of appropriate means of discourse[245]. Broadly speaking, the subject makes no sense unless one is open-minded about dimensions of existence that reach beyond the self, and unless one is ready to talk seriously about such items as shared meanings, progress, timeless value, or even metaphysics.

I now wish to devote a few more remarks to the most fundamental dimension of the subject, such as it was already referred to at different places. What we find at that level is (i) an inquiry concerning future-oriented motivation: does'nt that sort of motivation imply a background trust in the durability of human life and culture which eludes clear articulation? (cf.5.2 above); (ii) an inquiry concerning the resources of metaphysical speculation for bringing that background dimension within the circle of philosophical discourse, and for facing squarely the "why" of concern for the survival of mankind (cf.2.5 above on macro-ethics).

(i) I suggested that confidence in the durability of human affairs (i.e. in the indefinite "ongoingness" of history) forms a background dimension that is always *there* and always wider than what concretely inspires us to look forward in time — a temporal horizon that is at the always receding edge of our vision. Now I think it is a capital challenge for philosophy to reflect upon this status of certain dimensions of existence being given, and so always prior to human action and its search for reasons. Such dimensions could be termed existential conditions of meaning, underlying the world of identifiable goods, of meaningful objects of will. We cannot say "why" we naturally trust in humanity carrying on within an indefinitely open temporal horizon: the question would presuppose, erroneously, that the issue is one of means and ends. The only thing we can say, perhaps, is that this horizon conditions meaning by offering to our experience of the good the unlimited temporal

---

[245] Cf.Taylor 1989, 9 on the frequent lack of fit between what people "officially" and consciously believe, and what they need to make sense of their moral reactions.

space which it demands[246]. It is one of the paradoxes of the age that technology provides us with the means to put the survival of humanity at risk, drawing it so within the circle of that which we can decide upon, whereas our confidence in the perpetuity of mankind constitutionally resists giving reasons for itself: its status, fundamentally, is to be self-evident.

I think it would be possible here to draw an analogy with recent problems in bio-ethics, as many people feel that the development of science and technology gives us power over aspects of life which intrinsically refuse to be subjected to human will. Although such feelings prove incapable of generating precise limits for scientific research and medical practice (new frontiers are crossed every day), I think they reveal an awareness of the finite character of our human condition: a condition that cannot be manipulated at will without a major loss of meaning.

I mentioned bio-ethics; still another context where that experience of the intrinsic "givenness" of things plays a central role is, of course, the ecological one. The whole ecological movement can be understood as the search for such an outside dimension: nature in the sense of all that which we rejoice in because we don't control it. There are many things which we value because they are gifts — because they are there to be received, and not made, or taken.

It is perhaps tempting for the modern naturalist temper to explain the feeling that one is dealing with a dimension that is always "already there" (a dimension which cannot be questioned itself) by claiming that one is making the mistake of interrogating the brute survival instinct of the species. I think this would be a philosophically dubious step. Is there a survival instinct in the human species (as contrasted with the survival instinct of the individual human being?). What experiment would we need in order to find out? A better point of view consists in considering ourselves as beings deeply determined by factors located on the level of mind, a merely "vital" infrastructure being therefore difficult to identify (as is suggested by the continuous debate on "nature" vs."culture" in anthropology).

(ii) I have interpreted an open temporal horizon for mankind as a condition of meaning, and so as prior to any giving of reasons. I now must concede that this interpretation has taken no account of metaphysical argument: does

---

[246] So that the dimension of time, as related to the world of values, could be considered to share the *a priori* character which Kant attributes to space and time in sensory experience.

philosophical discourse have resources to overcome the resistance of the subject to any sort of explanation?

Let me mention, as an already classical instance of the metaphysical approach, Hans Jonas' "Imperative of responsibility" (1984). Jonas starts by defining a principle of responsibility which prescribes that we must anticipate the consequences of our actions in their full temporal extent (see 2.5). He then explains this principle by basing it on a still higher norm stipulating that the existence of Man on this planet (Man as a free moral agent) must not be endangered. The doors of history must be kept open. But why should they? It is here, of course, that Jonas' reasoning faces a crucial challenge. His argument is a difficult and highly abstract one: he justifies the fundamental norm just referred to by reading an ontological implication in the idea of Man. This idea, he says, does intrinsically call for its embodiment in reality; it does so for Jonas within the context of a philosophy of life and evolution which places Man at the top of Life considered as a process of self-affirmation which fundamentally denies the separation of "ought" from "is".

These few lines may suffice to convince the reader of the difficulty of *arguing* for the perpetuity of mankind. I cannot attempt to discuss Jonas' reasoning at this place. It forms a lofty and lonely monument within the contemporary philosophical landscape, which few philosophers dare to approach[247]. It is interesting to note that the only philosophical competition Jonas himself deals with (and he does so by a forceful rejection) is the marxist idea of History finding its justification in the march towards a final end state which would leave nothing to be desired and so would overstep, in effect, our human condition. The general reader here finds himself on safer ground: Jonas joins the many critics of Utopia, in the name of human liberty. No period of history "stands nearer to God" than any other, as the German historian Ranke expressed it — a proposition which does'nt exclude modest, non-totalitarian conceptions of progress. There is a fundamental divide between having a sense of direction and endowing that direction with messianic attributes. So it is not from within our conception of history that we should expect some proof of mankind's ultimate necessity. That proof is looked for by Jonas on the level of a general metaphysics of life and evolution, where human freedom and creativity stands at the top.

---

[247] The only other philosopher I am aware of, who also attempts to develop up a secular argument for the survival of mankind (based on the philosophy of discourse) is K.O.Apel (1988).

When discussing macro-ethics, I put the following question: if we collectively assume responsibility for the negative consequences of our way of life, to whom do we owe that responsibility? If we centre that question not only on a just distribution of environmental resources across time, but also on the background issue of the survival of mankind, the answer is no easy one. We saw that Jonas tries out a metaphysical answer: responsibility is due to the essence of Man, because that essence itself calls for Man's presence on earth. Jonas himself is quite aware of the difficulty of his attempt. Religious belief has answers here which philosophy must still seek "with uncertain propects of success". Faith in revealed truth can supply the foundation for ethics, "but it is not there on command... Metaphysics on the other hand has always been a business of reason, and reason can be set to work upon demand."[248]

But then I think we should face the following paradox. If we consider the metaphysical attempt to be a hopeless one (and the difficulty of Jonas' argument may tempt many of his readers to conclude exactly that), to what or to whom do we regard our collective assumption of responsibility to be due? The very concept of responsibility carries the implication that an authority exists that may call us to account. Does it make sense to conceive that authority as being mankind itself, under an empty sky? That would resemble the famous baron Münchhausen who pulled himself out of a swamp by pulling at his own hair.

As I see it, this is one of the many places in philosophy where we simply have to admit that human reason points beyond itself.

---

[248] Jonas 1984, 45.

CHAPTER 6

JUSTICE AS FOCUS

Golding's classic argument retains its full provocative power: the future generations

> "comprise the community of the future, a community with which we cannot expect to share a common life. It appears to me that the more remote the members of this community are, the more problematic our obligations to them become ... .One might go so far as to say that if we have an obligation to distant future generations it is an obligation not to plan for them. Not only do we not know their conditions of life, we also do not know whether they will maintain the same (or a similar) conception of the good life for man as we do." So we should be content with caring for our immediate posterity: "it should be unwise, both from an ethical and a practical perspective, to seek to promote the good of the very distant."[249]

This of course is something the present argument denies by virtue of its initial premise; we cannot stay content with caring for our immediate posterity, all future generations have a claim on the resources of the planet. But Golding's argument works as a useful background reminder of our lack of knowledge and of the ambitious character of the hold on the future which justice between generations is asking for. The following remarks I devote to a central difficulty, already noted frequently in previous pages: the historically situated character of our judgment, and the impact on those judgments of our awareness of historical change. That difficulty affects both the definition of what justice itself wants us to aim for (cf.2.2 above, the discussion of the sustainable economy) and the confidence we have in the ongoing validity of the values that support a concern with the welfare of future generations (cf.5.2.1 above).

After having remarked on that difficulty, I turn towards a reaffirmation of the postulate of intergenerational justice, and I end this chapter with a short comment on the issue of parochialism.

***

---

[249] Golding 1972, 96f

The detached point of view that is inherent in justice between generations easily connects with contemporary relativist pre-conceptions. Since the 18th century, we think of ourselves as being, collectively, on the march. With the demise of the idea of progress, that conviction of being engaged in a process of continuous historical change has, in a sense, become even stronger. For the future, for us, is more unpredictable than ever: we have few shared images of future society, because the dynamics of science and technology develop along lines we cannot foresee. So we think it is highly probable that people living some hundred (or already some fifty) years from now will have ways of life vastly different from ours. We just have to recall how many aspects of contemporary life could not have been predicted by people living in 1900. This makes us aware, at the same time, of ourselves being governed by cultural pre-conceptions which must inevitably colour our judgments about prospective states of affairs.

But historical relativism competes in our minds with our constitutive attachment to certain values — values we believe in — although it makes us suspect at the same time that these values are subject to an unpredictable evolution. In his criticism of the ethereal, cosmopolitan self of liberal deontology, Sandel highlights

> "those loyalties and convictions whose moral force consists partly in the fact that living by them is inseparable from understanding ourselves as the particular persons we are — as members of this family or community or nation or people, as bearers of this history, as sons and daughters of that revolution, as citizens of this republic ... ..(to) have character is to know that I move in a history I neither summon nor command, which carries consequences none the less for my choice and conduct."[250]

We are the victims of a fundamental schizophrenia, which consists in being committed, as the persons we are, to certain reasons for action — in not being able to think about them differently than we do (nor wishing to do so) — while being attracted at the same time, on the level of our general views of the world, by a sceptical attitude in respect of all claims on perpetuity.

The committed part of ourselves feeds a correspondingly committed position in regard to the future; we wish to fashion the future as much as we possibly can. According to O'Neill, our primary responsibility is to attempt, as far as it is possible, to ensure that future generations do belong to a community

---

[250] Sandel 1982, 179.

with ourselves[251]. In his 1988 study on the economy of the earth, Sagoff argues that our moral responsibility with regard to the future is not "a responsibility *to* the future as much as it is a responsibility *for* the future". The major decisions we make

> "determine ... what future people are like and what their preferences and tastes will be"[252].

But relativism does'nt disarm, and it surely wins in respect of remote periods. Who would dare to predict the ways of life of our descendants in the year 3000? In giving the fullest scope to this sort of scepticism, the detached view in a way undermines its own chances. Confidence in the values we hold is weakened by a belief in the temporary character of all things human; in the end, the detached view stands alone without external support. History may carry consequences for my choice and conduct, as Sandel says, but in the absence of any common sense of direction, what "history" seems to do is to make these consequences depend on a quite inscrutable network of causes and conditions. What is left is a sheer sense of the transience of things.

***

Whatever force we may concede to sceptical views concerning our hold on the future, I think it is morally impossible, at least in our present context of inquiry, to follow Golding's recommendation to care only for our immediate posterity. To my mind, the intuitive premise that the planet is not "ours" only — that its resources belong to the whole of mankind such as it extends across the ages — finds a solid foundation in the moral point of view, and and once the fundamentally time-related structure of the world of values has been brought to light. That intuitive premise has moreover become a living part of contemporary practice, through the concept of the sustainable society. So I have claimed that it must share the priority which John Rawls attributes in his theory to the just basic structure.

I here must express my disagreement with a remark made by O'Neill. He says that when the question of obligations to future generations is posed in terms of abstract obligation to possible future people who are strangers to us, this "is premised on the lack of a sense of continuity of the present with both

---

[251] O'Neill 1993, 34.

[252] Sagoff 1988, 63 (underl. by the author).

past and future"[253]. I do not think myself that the clear affirmation of a principle of justice that vetoes generational egoism shows any such relation with a deficient sense of continuity. In aiming to neutralize the power disequilibrium between the present and the future, it meets a structural problem of relations between generations that one needs to deal with in a general way: the impersonal character of the principle is essential to it[254]. One might add that it articulates an objectivity across time that is implicit in the experience of goods having a continued validity from one generation to another (cf.4.4.1). And once it has been put into place, the principle of justice itself forms no obstacle (on the contrary) to seeking support for its forward-looking orientation in all values that inspire a concern for the future beyond our individual life span.

It is true, I think, but unavoidable at the same time, that the detached view of justice, its refusal to confer a particular status to the interests of the living because of their position in time, sets the stage for our historicist pre-conceptions, and so tends to undermine itself the motivational support it can draw from values in other spheres than its own. I said that confidence in those values we hold presently is weakened by a belief in the temporary character of all things human. But a relevant question, it seems to me, is whether that belief, because of its abstract character, actually has the full corrosive effects one might imagine it to have on first reflection: we are convinced of the transience of everything, but we have no concrete images of what the future will bring.

The issue of historical relativism in a sense boils down to the following: whether we really can integrate into our decision-making the sort of scepticism which that relativism inspires.

A conceptual approach that can be tried out for dealing with that issue consists in splitting (so to speak) the future in two. I already mentioned the idea of a two-phased approach to the future (cf.2.2 above). Forecast and planning on the basis of an all-round and contemporary conception of the good life would be allowed within a prospective time-frame limited to "proximate" generations, while decisions concerning further periods would have to be taken within the "thin" framework of preventing life-threatening harms and irreversible ecospace losses. Something analogous is proposed by Avner de-Shalit, although in a confusing fashion: "justice" between generations is equated with the particular understandings of a specific community, which

---

[253] O'Neill 1993, 38.

[254] It is true that O'Neill, ibid. 52-56, also explicitly rejects "pure-time preferences".

should govern concern with the more proximate future, while it is an ad-
herence to merely "humanitarian" obligations that should rule our decisions in
respect of states of affairs after community has "faded away" (de-Shalit
does'nt say how we should predict the latter event)[255]. This model carries into
the future generations context a very Walzerian distinction between "justice",
denoting the obligations one has within a community, and the "humanitarian"
duty not to harm "strangers"[256].

The point of view I have developed myself in this book is the opposite one
that justice is a virtue which moral reason wants us to apply (by aiming at a
sustainable use of environmental resources) to our relations with the indefinite
sequence of future generations, quite independently of social conditions of any
sort, "community" belonging not to the sphere of justice itself but to the
sphere of contextual values whose outside help we may invoke (with varying
success) in order to strengthen, against many psychological obstacles, the
forward-looking attitude that inheres in justice to future generations.

Moreover, one wonders whether a neat separation can be drawn between a
"thin" definition of environmental harm, neutral from a cultural point of view,
and a "full" definition that has no inhibitions in the latter respect. It is true, and
that is the most direct rejoinder one can oppose to Golding's argument, that
there is a minimum or baseline zone of environmental harms that one cannot
imagine to depend on time-bound values. We don't have to speculate about
forming either or not a moral community with our descendants in order to
know that the disappearance of the ozone layer, the warming of the
atmosphere, or the uncontrolled dumping of nuclear waste carry major risks
for the welfare of future persons. Beyond that, however, there is a large
twilight zone where judgment is more or less strongly dependent on
conceptions of the good life. Can one expect decision-makers to take account
of that (in the way proposed by the two-phased approach) by anticipating an
unforeseeable "fading away" of those conceptions? For instance, the forecast
of future needs in the field of energy is surely related to sustaining the levels
of comfort, mobility, general welfare etc. which condition the opportunities
we consider to belong to a decent way of life. It does'nt anticipate some return
to pre-industrial times (nor could it of course because of population numbers).

---

[255] Cf.de-Shalit 1995, 51f.

[256] Ibid., 63: remote generations are compared with "strangers". I criticized such a
comparison in section 5.1.2. See also section 4.1 for a criticism of the "humanitarian"
approach.

And when we make long-term decisions about planting forests, conserving a natural habitat etc., we dont't consider anticipating (how?) some future disappearance of public interest in our natural environment. We have to trust in our own lights, and try to shape the future according to our present beliefs. There simply is what one might call a fundamental historical risk, in being together immersed in history.

***

As it turns our eyes towards remote regions of time, justice between generations may appear to require from us a too ambitious hold on the future. But it also makes quite serious demands in another dimension, the dimension of generality. What I mean is that the problems we face in the sphere of the environment tend to have a global dimension. Justice between generations, considered as a value which calls for a definition in very impersonal terms, cannot find the right support for its forward-looking stance in values that that have a parochial character and therefore lack a sufficient measure of consensus on the world level. We live in a world of many nations, cultures, loyalties, and our interest in the future is often rooted in a love of "persons and places" (Passmore). One wonders whether the communitarian thinkers, who are so helpful for making us aware of the intergenerational scope of many values in the first place, pay sufficient attention to the price that is sometimes paid for this in terms of universal validity ("my country, right or wrong"). What one is facing here is the potentially divisive aspect of solidarity. On the one hand, feelings of solidarity may cause us to sacrifice our interests to those of future people, but on the other hand, those feelings, because of their parochial nature, may not be on a level with (or may even be contrary to) the global commitment which environmental problems structurally demand.

So I think that within our present context of discussion, the theory of justice must resist an approach like Walzer's, which links the concept of justice to local understandings, unless more thought is spent on the ways and means of an inter-cultural meeting of minds. As Jeremy Waldron formulates it in an article on the "cosmopolitan alternative", the localism of Walzer's approach would be catastrophic for many of the global issues we face. What we need is community on a global scale, "a bringing together of a diversity of perspectives and ideas in the formation of common solutions to common problems"[257].

A similar comment can be made about Avner de-Shalit's position, which lets the content of justice reflect, primarily, obligations that are internal to a specific community. I think such a position goes against the grain of what the present world situation is asking for; at least it doesn't set the right priorities.

In his book on future generations, Birnbacher suggests that for the time being, it would be quite unrealistic to expect a general extension of future-oriented concern beyond the limits of one's own national or cultural group[258]. I think he is too pessimistic about that, considering the rapid growth of world-wide contacts between people in all sorts of fields. And what about global aims such as scientific research, the rule of law on a world level, the dialogue between the great world religions, or the conservation of the great monuments of mankind? Anyhow, his argument is an interesting one. Let us imagine an environmental issue arising on a global or at least regional level, which resists the separate targeting, by each country, of "its" future population. And let us assume, in the countries involved, a motivational deficit: it proves to be difficult to generate a consensus on measures at the required scale, because their adoption presupposes feelings of solidarity with a much wider future constituency than one's own. Now, it might be argued that this deficit can be lessened by *caring by proxy* for the future members of other groups: let us help their *present* members to care for them, without asking ourselves whether we share that concern. This certainly is an attractive line of reasoning, but one wonders how far it is getting us. What is our motive for helping those present members of other groups in their future-oriented concerns in the first place? Justice supplies a motive: we can conceive a duty to help one another in being just to future generations (North-South relations here particularly come to mind). Once justice is supposed to govern our actions, caring by proxy certainly helps with curing its possible motivational deficiency. But the context in which Birnbacher presents the issue is the more pessimistic one of a lack of psychological support that endangers the taking of any action at the required level at all, whatever the weak promptings of justice may be. How do we get to be interested in the welfare of future persons beyond our own constituency? Now I think that if we assume that we don't have the slightest interest in the fate of those "other" future persons, it is assumed at the same

---

[257] Waldron 1995, 126.

[258] Birnbacher 1988, 219, 229-230.

time that we don't share, on a basis of solidarity, any forward-looking values with the presently living members of the relevant groups. There is no *common* interest in the future at all. But the only reason I then can imagine for helping the present members of other groups in their forward-looking concerns is the expectation that they will help *us* when the occasion arises. The expectation of reciprocity provides the motive. But I wonder whether this line of reasoning doesn't act as a boomerang. The environmental issue which one has agreed to consider as a global one (that was why a motivational deficit was observed to exist in the first place) is dealt with for motivational reasons by postulating separate "group" concerns with the future, within a framework of reciprocity, although the global nature of the issue makes such separate consideration a doubtful proposition from the start.

So we come back to the need for common values in order to support common action. We need to work for a worldwide conception of the shared interests of mankind. The final question posed by a theory of justice to future generations must be: how the idea of humanity as a single historical entity and of the earth as its common heritage can become a concrete reality in our minds.

It is true in many instances that countries or regions cannot hope to defend ecological interests they tend to identify from a "local" perspective unless they participate in schemes that work on the world level and thus help to create a global consciousness. Insofar, it is practice itself which may provide the necessary moral education.

BIBLIOGRAPHY

Achterberg, W.: 1994, *Samenleving, natuur en duurzaamheid*. Van Gorcum, Assen.

Achterberg, W.: 1990, 'Duurzaamheid en intrinsieke waarde', in *Wijsgerig Perspectief* 30/6 (1989/90), 169-175.

Apel, K.O.: 1988, *Diskurs und Verantwortung. Das Problem des Übergangs zur postkonventionellen Moral*. Suhrkamp, Frankfurt.

Asperen, G.M.van: 1993, 'Een temidden van velen'. In *Het bedachte leven (beschouwingen over maatschappij, zingeving en ethiek)*. Boom, Amsterdam.

Barry, B.: 1978, 'Circumstances of justice and future generations'. In R.I.Sikora and B.Barry (eds.), *Obligations to future generations*, 204-248. Temple University Press, Philadelphia.

Barry, B.: 1979, 'Justice as reciprocity'. In Kamenka (ed.), *Justice (Ideas and ideologies)*, 50-78. Arnold, London.

Barry, B.: 1989, *Theories of justice*. Harvester-Wheatsheaf, London.

Barry, B.: 1991, *Liberty and justice*. Clarendon Press, Oxford.

Beitz, Ch.: 1979, *Political theory and international relations*. Princeton University Press.

Bergson, Henri: 1955 (1932), *Les deux sources de la morale et de la religion*, Presses Universitaires de France, Paris.

Birnbacher, D.: 1988, *Verantwortung für zukünftige Generationen*. Reclam, Stuttgart.

Birnbacher B.: 1993, 'Qualität des Lebens und Verantwortung für zukünftige Generationen', in *An ethics of life in cultural contexts*, Jahresbericht 1993 (30.Jahrestagung), Societas Ethica.

Birnie, P.W. & Boyle, A.E.: 1992 (repr.with corr.1994), *International law and the environment*. Clarendon Press, Oxford.

Brown Weiss, E.: 1988, *In fairness to future generations*. UN University/ Transnational publishers, Tokyo & New York.

Comte-Sponville, André: 1995, *Petit traité des grandes vertus*, Presses Universitaires de France, Paris.

Cowen T. & Parfit D.: 1992, 'Against the social discount rate'. In *Justice between age groups and generations* (Laslett P. & Fishkin J. eds.), 144-161. Yale University Press.

Daly, H.E. and Cobb Jr.,J.B.: 1989, *For the common good*. Beacon Press, Boston.

Dante Alighieri: 1904, *Inferno*. Dent & Co (The Temple Classics), London.

Delsol, Ch.: 1994, 'Les pensées de la nature et la question du temps', in *Philosophie politique* no.6.

de-Shalit, A.: 1995, *Why posterity matters*. Routledge, London & New York.

Epstein, R.A.: 1992, 'Justice across the generations'. In *Justice between age groups and generations* (Laslett P. & Fishkin J. eds.), 84-106. Yale University Press.

Feinberg, J.: 1980, 'The rights of animals and unborn generations'. In *Rights, justice and the bounds of liberty*, 159-184. Princeton University Press.

Finnis, J.: 1980, *Natural law and natural rights*. Clarendon Press, Oxford.

Fried, Ch.: 1970, *An anatomy of values (Problems of personal and social choice)*. Harvard University Press.

Fuller, Lon L.: 1964, *The morality of law*. Yale University Press, New Haven & London.

Glover, J.: 1977, *Causing death and saving lives*. Penguin books.

Golding, M.P.: 1972, Obligations to future generations. In *Monist* 56 (1972).

Goodin, R.E.: 1985, *Protecting the vulnerable*. University of Chicago Press, Chicago.

Hart, H.L.A.: 1961, *The concept of law*. Clarendon Press, Oxford.

van Hengel, E. en Gremmen B.: 1995, 'Milieugebruiksruimte: tussen natuurwet en conventie', in *Kennis en methode*, jg.XIX 1995-3.

Hilhorst, M.T.: 1987, *Verantwoordelijk voor toekomstige generaties?* Kok, Kampen.

Hume, D.: 1767, 'An enquiry concerning the principles of morals', in *Essays and treatises on several subjects*, Vol.II. Millar (London) & Kincaid/Donaldson (Edinburgh).

Jonas, H.: 1974, 'Change and permanence: On the possibility of understanding history'. In *Philosophical essays*, 237-260. University of Chicago Press, Chicago-London.

Jonas, H.: 1974, 'Contemporary problems in ethics from a Jewish perspective'. In *Philosophical essays*, 168-184. University of Chicago Press, Chicago-London.

Jonas, H.: 1984 (1979), *The imperative of responsibility (In search of an ethics for the technological age)*. University of Chicago Press, Chicago-London.

Jonas, H.: 1996, 'Immortality and the modern temper'. In *Mortality and morality (A search for the good after Auschwitz)*. Northwestern University Press, Evanston (Ill.)

Laslett, P. and Fishkin, J.S: 1972, 'Introduction: Processional Justice'. In *Justice between age groups and generations*, 1-23. Yale University Press, New Haven & London.

Laslett, P.: 1972, 'Is there a generational contract', In *Justice between age groups and generations*, 24-47. Yale University Press, New Haven & London.

Meyer, L.: 1997, 'More than they have a right to: future people and our future oriented projects'. In *Contingent future persons*, 137-151. Kluwer Academic Publishers, Dordrecht/Boston/London.

Mulhall, S. and Swift, A.: 1996, *Liberals & communitarians* (2nd ed.). Blackwell, Oxford.

MacIntyre, A.: 1984, *After virtue* (2nd ed.). University of Notre Dame Press, Notre Dame, Indiana.

Marx K. and Engels F.: 1998 (1848), *The communist manifesto*. Oxford World's Classics, Oxford University Press.

Musschenga B.: 1993, 'Are health and quality of life culturally relative', in *An ethics of life in cultural contexts*, Jahresbericht 1993 (30.Jahrestagung), Societas Ethica.

Nagel, Th.: 1986, *The view from nowhere*. Oxford University Press.

Nagel, Th.: 1991, *Equality and partiality*. Oxford University Press.

Nieuwenhuis J.H.: 1997, 'Zij die geboren worden groeten U', in *Confrontatie & compromis (recht, retoriek en burgerlijke moraal)*, 123-137. Kluwer, Deventer.

Norton, B.: 1989, 'Intergenerational equity and environmental decisions: a model using Rawls' veil of ignorance', in *Ecological economics* Vol.1 no.2, 137-159.

O'Neill, J.: 1993, *Ecology, policy and politics*. Routledge, London & New York.

Opschoor, H.: 1989, *Na ons geen zondvloed*. Kok Agora, Kampen.

Opschoor, H.: 1996, 'Sustainable growth and employment', in *The ecumenical review*, vol.48 nr.3, July 1996, 332-344.

Ost, François: 1985, 'Les multiples temps du droit'. In *Le droit et le futur* (Actes du IIIe colloque de l'Association française de philosophie du droit). Presses Universitaires de France, Paris.

Ost, François: 1995, *La nature hors la loi, l'écologie à l'épreuve du droit*. La Découverte, Paris.

Page, T.: 1991, 'Sustainability and the problem of valuation', in *Ecological economics* (ed.R.Costanza), 58-74. Columbia University Press, New York.

Parfit, D.: 1984, *Reasons and persons*. Clarendon Press, Oxford.

Partridge, E.: 1981, 'Why care about the future'. In *Responsibilities for future generations* (E.Partridge ed.). Prometheus books, Buffalo.

Passmore, J.: 1970, *The perfectibility of man*. Duckworth, London.

Passmore, J.: 1974, *Man's responsibility for nature*. Charles Scribner's sons, New York.

Paterson, M.: 1996, 'International justice and global warming'. In *The Ethical dimensions of global change* (B.Holden ed.). MacMillan Press Ltd, London.

Plater, Z.J.B., Abrams R.H. and Goldfarb W.: 1992, *Environmental law and policy: a coursebook on nature, law and society*. West publishing Company, St.Paul.

Postema, G., *On the moral presence of our past* (unpubl.paper)

Pot, J.H. van der: 1985, *Die Bewertung des technischen Fortschritts (Eine systematische Übersicht der Theorien)*. Van Gorcum, Assen.

Rawls, J.: 1971, *A theory of justice*. Oxford University Press.

Rawls, J.: 1993, *Political liberalism*. Columbia University Press, New York.

Raz, J.: 1986, *The morality of freedom*. Clarendon Press, Oxford.

Ricoeur, P.: 1955, 'Le socius et le prochain'. In *Histoire et vérité*, 213-229. Editions du Seuil, Paris.

Ricoeur, P.: 1990, *Soi-même comme un autre*. Editions du Seuil, Paris.

Sagoff, M.: 1988, *The economy of the earth*. Cambridge University Press.

Saladin, P. and Zenger, C.A.: 1988, *Rechte künftiger Generationen*. Helbing & Lichtenhahn Verlag, Basel/Frankfurt a.M.

Sandel, M.: 1982, *Liberalism and the limits of justice*. Cambridge University Press, Cambridge.

Sands, P.: 1995, *Principles of international environmental law,* Vol.1. Manchester University Press, Manchester/New York.

Shue, H.: 1992, 'The unavoidability of justice', in *The International politics of the environment* (A.Hurrell and B.Kingsbury eds.), 373-397. Oxford University Press.

Singer, B.A.: 1988, 'An extension of Rawls' theory of justice to environmental ethics', in *Environmental ethics*, Vol.10 (1988), 217-231.

Steiner, G.: 1971, *In Bluebeard's castle (some notes towards the redefinition of culture)*. Yale University Press, New Haven.

Taylor, Ch.:1989, *Sources of the self*. Cambridge University Press.

Wal, G.A.van der: 1979, *De zorg voor lateren: van later zorg?* (inaugural adress Rotterdam 1979).

Wal, G.A.van der: 1996, ''In praise of moralism'. Pleidooi voor eerherstel van een verwaarloosde vorm van ethiekbeoefening'. In *De omkering van de wereld*, 161-170. Ambo, Baarn.

Waldron J.: 1995, 'Minority cultures and the cosmopolitan alternative'. In *Nation, state and the coexistence of different communities* (T.van Wiiligenburg, F.R.Heeger & W.van der Burg eds.). Kok Pharos Publishing House, Kampen.

Walzer M.: 1983, *Spheres of justice (A defence of pluralism and equality)*. Blackwell, Oxford.

Wetenschappelijke raad voor het regeringsbeleid: 1994, *Duurzame risico's: een blijvend gegeven*. (Rapporten aan de regering 44). Sdu Uitgeverij, den Haag.

Willigenburg, T.van: 1996, 'De subjectiviteit van leven-oordelen', in *Tijdschrift voor Gezondheidsrecht* nr.5/1996, 252-269.

World Commission on Environment and Development (WCED): 1987, *Our Common Future*. Oxford University Press.

World Commission on Environment and Development (Experts group on environmental law of the ---): 1987, *Environmental protection and sustainable development (Legal principles and recommendations)*. Graham & Trotman/Martinus Nijhoff, London/Dordrecht/Boston.

INDEX

articulation (of values), 118-119

Barry,B., 2, 9, 59, 61, 62, 76f., 90f.
baseline concept, 19, 21, 33, 54, 157
Bergson, H., 96
Beitz, Ch., 55
Birnbacher, D., 20, 159

chain of love, 47-48, 121-122
circumstances of justice, 59, 65, 76-77,
    92-97
coexistence (justice and --) 59, 65, 103-
    110
common heritage of mankind, 34-35
community (and communitarian theory),
    119, 125-128, 136, 154, 157
culture (contemporary --), 120, 133f.,
    139-142

Delsol, Ch., 37
de-Shalit, A., 121-123, 125, 156-157, 159
democracy 32
discounting future states of affairs, 81-82,
    86-87

ecological thought, 36-37
ecospace, 18
environment (general features), 4, 16, 35,
    42-43
Epstein, R.A., 114
equal opportunities, 21, 90, 95

Feinberg, J., 49-50
Fishkin, J.S., 44-45, 91
Fried, Ch., 83
Fuller, L., 62
future generations:

concept of 43-45
our relations with (general features),
    11, 46-48, 53, 94, 99-101, 111-112
strangers? 108-110

Glover, J., 82, 85, 112
Golding, M.P., 153, 157, 159
Goodin, R.E., 96
good (see value)
Gremmen, B., 20

van Hengel, E., 20
harm, 57
history
    cultural/historical relativity of our
    values, 19f., 120, 129f., 140f., 153f.
human rights, 27
    a h.right to an adequate environment?
    27-28, 30 n.42
Hume, 76, 93f., 104

indeterminacy of justice, 8, 25, 55
individuals
    justice between generations is justice
    to -- ,
    45, 51, 53, 91-92, 121
intergenerational cooperation, 119-120,
    128-133, 147
Jonas, H., 40-41, 115, 126, 134, 151-152
just basic structure, 3-8, 28-29, 52, 64
    regulative primacy of, 4-5, 6 n.10, 6-7,
    26, 28, 29-34, 54, 90-91
justice, *see* also Rawls
    concept of, 4, 52-54
    structures across time of, 59-63
    socially corrective (counterfactual)
    power, 11, 53, 56, 59, 93f., 105
    and coexistence, 103-110
justice to future generations

Law and Philosophy Library

1. E. Bulygin, J.-L. Gardies and I. Niiniluoto (eds.): *Man, Law and Modern Forms of Life*. With an Introduction by M.D. Bayles. 1985 ISBN 90-277-1869-5

2. W. Sadurski: *Giving Desert Its Due*. Social Justice and Legal Theory. 1985 ISBN 90-277-1941-1

3. N. MacCormick and O. Weinberger: *An Institutional Theory of Law*. New Approaches to Legal Positivism. 1986 ISBN 90-277-2079-7

4. A. Aarnio: *The Rational as Reasonable*. A Treatise on Legal Justification. 1987 ISBN 90-277-2276-5

5. M.D. Bayles: *Principles of Law*. A Normative Analysis. 1987 ISBN 90-277-2412-1; Pb: 90-277-2413-X

6. A. Soeteman: *Logic in Law*. Remarks on Logic and Rationality in Normative Reasoning, Especially in Law. 1989 ISBN 0-7923-0042-4

7. C.T. Sistare: *Responsibility and Criminal Liability*. 1989 ISBN 0-7923-0396-2

8. A. Peczenik: *On Law and Reason*. 1989 ISBN 0-7923-0444-6

9. W. Sadurski: *Moral Pluralism and Legal Neutrality*. 1990 ISBN 0-7923-0565-5

10. M.D. Bayles: *Procedural Justice*. Allocating to Individuals. 1990 ISBN 0-7923-0567-1

11. P. Nerhot (ed.): *Law, Interpretation and Reality*. Essays in Epistemology, Hermeneutics and Jurisprudence. 1990 ISBN 0-7923-0593-0

12. A.W. Norrie: *Law, Ideology and Punishment*. Retrieval and Critique of the Liberal Ideal of Criminal Justice. 1991 ISBN 0-7923-1013-6

13. P. Nerhot (ed.): *Legal Knowledge and Analogy*. Fragments of Legal Epistemology, Hermeneutics and Linguistics. 1991 ISBN 0-7923-1065-9

14. O. Weinberger: *Law, Institution and Legal Politics*. Fundamental Problems of Legal Theory and Social Philosophy. 1991 ISBN 0-7923-1143-4

15. J. Wróblewski: *The Judicial Application of Law*. Edited by Z. Bańkowski and N. MacCormick. 1992 ISBN 0-7923-1569-3

16. T. Wilhelmsson: *Critical Studies in Private Law*. A Treatise on Need-Rational Principles in Modern Law. 1992 ISBN 0-7923-1659-2

17. M.D. Bayles: *Hart's Legal Philosophy*. An Examination. 1992 ISBN 0-7923-1981-8

18. D.W.P. Ruiter: *Institutional Legal Facts*. Legal Powers and their Effects. 1993 ISBN 0-7923-2441-2

19. J. Schonsheck: *On Criminalization*. An Essay in the Philosophy of the Criminal Law. 1994 ISBN 0-7923-2663-6

20. R.P. Malloy and J. Evensky (eds.): *Adam Smith and the Philosophy of Law and Economics*. 1994 ISBN 0-7923-2796-9

21. Z. Bańkowski, I. White and U. Hahn (eds.): *Informatics and the Foundations of Legal Reasoning*. 1995 ISBN 0-7923-3455-8

Law and Philosophy Library

KLUWER ACADEMIC PUBLISHERS – DORDRECHT / BOSTON / LONDON